CRYSTAL CLEAR
stories of hope

Published by Crystal Meth Anonymous, Inc. © 2011

CONTENTS

FOREWORD

THE FIRST MEETING OF CRYSTAL METH ANONYMOUS WAS HELD IN WEST Hollywood, California, in 1994, and since that time our fellowship has grown to include groups in thirty-three states and four countries. Because of the success of our fellowship, we now feel it is time to share our experiences with other crystal meth addicts, especially those who do not live close enough to attend our meetings.

In 1935, two alcoholics had a conversation in Akron, Ohio, that started a revolution in the treatment of addictive diseases. Although their fellowship dealt specifically with alcoholism, the Twelve Steps of their program have proved successful in dealing with other problems as well. As stated in the foreword to *Alcoholics Anonymous*: "We are sure that our way of living has its advantages for all." For crystal meth addicts, that has certainly been true, and we, the members of Crystal Meth Anonymous, present this book as a testament to that fact.

Many other books have been written with instructions for working through the Twelve Steps. We are not attempting that feat here. Instead, we hope that crystal meth addicts will identify with the stories and experiences in this book, and that many will decide to explore our fellowship further.

Before coming to CMA, many of us did not think we had a problem with crystal meth, while others knew we had a problem but did not believe recovery was possible. Hearing the stories of other crystal meth addicts proved to us we had the same problem, and, as we watched them recover, we came to believe the fellowship could work for us as well.

If you think you may have a problem with crystal meth, we suggest you read through this book with an open mind, and, if you live close enough, attend one of our meetings. Our fellowship has worked for thousands of addicts, and we believe it can work for you, too.

—*Saturday, January 8, 2011*

ARE YOU A TWEAKER?

The reading "Are You a Tweaker?" was written by one of our early members for a meeting started in March 2000. The reading was written to give CMA members something with which to identify. "Are You a Tweaker?" began as something exclusive to that early meeting but soon became popular and cherished by CMA members all over the country. It was voted in as the first Conference Approved reading by the CMA General Services Conference in Park City, Utah, on October 19, 2008.

IT DOESN'T MATTER WHAT YOU CALL IT. IT DOESN'T MATTER HOW YOU DID IT. It brought us to our knees, because without exception that's what it does.

Is speed a problem in your life? Are you an addict? Only you can answer those questions. For most of us who have admitted defeat, the answer is very clear. Yes, we had a problem with speed, and no, we couldn't fix the problem by ourselves. We had to admit defeat to win. Speed was our master.

We couldn't control our drug use. What started out as weekend or occasional use became daily use, and we soon found ourselves beyond human aid. We truly suffered from a lack of power to fix our problem.

Some of us used speed as a tool to work harder and longer, but we couldn't keep a job. Others picked at their faces and arms for hours and hours or pulled out their hair. Some of us had uncontrollable sexual desire.

Others endlessly tinkered with projects, accomplishing nothing, but found ourselves so busy we couldn't get to work on time.

We deluded ourselves into thinking that staying up for nights on end was OK, that our tweaking was under control, and that we could quit if we wanted to, or that we couldn't afford to quit, or that our using didn't affect our lives. Maybe we saw a friend go to jail, or lose their apartment, or lose their job, or lose the trust of their family, or die, but our clouded minds wouldn't admit we were next.

Most of us saw no way out, believing that we would use until the day we died. Almost universally, if we had an honest moment, we found that our drug use made seemingly insurmountable problems in our lives. The only way out was if we had the courage to admit that speed, our onetime friend, was killing us.

It doesn't matter how you got here. The courts sent some of us, others came for family or friends, and some of us came to CMA on our own. The question is, if you want help and are willing to go to any lengths to change your life.

OUR BILL'S STORY

The following account describes how one of the original members of Crystal Meth Anonymous found sobriety. In CMA, we generally try to tell our own stories instead of recounting those of other people, but at the time of this writing our friend had recently been diagnosed with cancer and was unable to write it himself. He gave us permission to adapt a transcript of one of the several recordings of his talks and reviewed it for accuracy. He has since passed away, and our debt of gratitude to him can never be repaid. We humbly submit this retelling, with our eternal thanks.

MY NAME IS BILL, AND I AM A CRYSTAL METH ADDICT.

I don't look like it today, but I am still a crystal meth addict. And this is the only place in the world where I can stand before a group of people and say that I'm a liar, a cheat, and a thief. And when I'm done everyone will say, "Wow, wasn't he great?" It's because the members of CMA understand all of that and know that it isn't really me. I'm always comfortable around a group of crystal meth addicts because I can do something stupid and everyone knows what that's about. We get room to grow here and become the person we were meant to be.

I'm supposed to tell what it was like, what happened, and what it's like now. Well, it used to be pretty bad. What happened was that it got worse. And now it's okay, thank you very much. That's pretty much how it went. I'll tell a little more about me, and then I'll also tell about the history of CMA and how it got started.

I was born in New England, a great place to grow up. Early on I was taught that the only thing that mattered was me: My clothes were the best, my eyelashes were the best—you name it. I was the first of a generation, and in my Irish-Russian family, that meant a lot. They wanted me to be a senator or a governor, but that didn't work out because I turned out to be gay. That can really make a mess of things.

I learned early on that I could lie and get things. My parents, aunts, and uncles would ask me how much I loved them, and I would say, "A football's worth." "A basketball's worth." "A pony's worth." "A car's worth." I got all those things, so I basically learned prostitution, not in the literal sense, but rather with the idea of using other people to get what I want. Later, that same behavior would apply to getting high: Every gift I had would be turned toward getting drugs, getting a little more high, getting you a little less high, and using you to get what I needed to stay far, far "out there."

At the age of 12 I was introduced to speed, in the form of meth tabs. I used to put a meth tab in a glass of water, then drink it and go off to school so I could slow down and catch up to everyone else. I drank, too. It started with my mother's port wine, which I would mix with grape juice so it would look the same, but I later found out I prefer scotch, gin, vodka, and tequila. Eventually, though, I discovered that if I took two of the meth tabs I would feel better, and if I took a whole lot of them I would feel a whole lot better—and I could study. I could concentrate at school, read my notes once, get an A, then go home and crash.

By the time I was 15, my parents (with the help of my doctor) had a drug addict on their hands, with uppers in the morning and downers at night. That pattern set in and stayed with me until I was 40 years old, except that it turned into uppers in the morning, then downers fifteen days later. I'm not sure how that happened, but I found that two or three days of being high were so-so, a week was okay, twelve days were better, but by fifteen days I could change the world. My friends and I would move the planets around and solve the world's problems, sitting in a bathhouse doing speed.

Then somewhere along the way, someone said to me, "You know, you can shoot those things." I thought, Why not? So, I tried it—nineteen of them. I had been high before, but I didn't really know about "high" until I started firing them up (injecting). When I ran out of meth tabs I would buy street crystal, and it became, without a doubt, the darkest place I've ever been. I was alone and homeless. Some of my friends would let me shower at their place and eat something, but they didn't let me stay there, so I would sleep in a Laundromat or a park.

I didn't understand, though, how unmanageable my life had become. One day a friend mentioned that a local celebrity was back in rehab and I made a joke that she had been shooting scotch this time. My friend said, "You can't shoot scotch whiskey," so I pulled out a syringe and did it. Another time I was sitting on a bus, all cleaned up (I thought), reading a paper. The man next to me said, "You had better go back to San Francisco. The fuzz will get you down here." I couldn't understand how he knew.

I don't want to get too caught up in the drug stories, but I do want to give you an idea of how far down I went. One time I got loaded and put on a yellow latex leotard with chain mail over it, then climbed a tree in the park, saying, "Chirp, chirp!" I wouldn't come down, either. The firemen had to come and remove me from the tree, but that's another story.

I made eight or nine attempts to stop cold turkey without success. Then one August morning, I was getting ready for my noon hit, and I couldn't get the needle in. I got frustrated and threw it away, but for some reason I didn't chase the high this time. Then twenty-four hours went by without drugs. Then another day went by. Then two weeks went by, and I started thinking, I can do this.

After a month, I was out in the mountains on a bike run when someone offered me a beer. I was about to drink it when I realized that if I took even one sip of that beer I would immediately be looking for whatever drugs I could find. I started shaking and didn't drink it. Later that night, I said the first prayer I had ever said that wasn't a bargain. I said, "Take me home," over and over.

But by that Christmas I was getting really drunk again. I had been staying with a friend of mine who was a bartender, and he would let me sweep the floor after he closed the bar, then give me some of his tips. We were walking to get something to eat when he pointed out a house that was sitting far off the street and said it was a recovery house for alcoholics and drug addicts. The remark passed me by completely. I didn't want to hear anything about that.

Strangely enough, about three days later I found myself knocking on their door. I was met by a man who was over 6 feet tall and weighed about 300 pounds. He looked down at me from what seemed like an enormous height and said, "Welcome home." I knew for the first time in my life that one of my prayers had been answered.

All over the walls were big posters: "The Twelve Steps," "The Twelve Traditions," "Easy Does It." As I looked at them, they seemed familiar. The nuns at school had taught me to trust in God, be kind to your neighbor, and love yourself, and that's what these Steps seemed to be saying. It's a little more complicated than that, but I still think that's what they're about.

The first three Steps direct my life in any future activity. I am powerless over drugs and alcohol, and my life was unmanageable. When I realized that, I had to ask for help, so there must be something to ask. That took me to Step Two, where I came to believe there is a Power greater than myself that could restore me to sanity. I didn't know yet what that Higher Power was, just that it was there and that it could keep me from using and drinking. That is something I am absolutely sure of today.

In Step Three I was asked to turn my will and my life over to the care of God as I understood Him. I couldn't believe they were actually asking me to give it all up, but when I looked back at my life, I saw that for the past thirty years I had totally surrendered to drugs. Drugs ruled my life absolutely. Everything I did was viewed through the lens of my addiction, and if it messed with my getting high, I didn't do it. They were asking me to surrender to a Power that could keep me sober and restore my life, so I did it.

Way at the other end I saw this other Step, Ten, that said to continue to take personal inventory and when I was wrong, promptly admit it. When am I ever wrong? Maybe two or three times since 1952, but otherwise it was always you. I would wake up some mornings having been beaten up the night before and couldn't figure out why, since I didn't do anything wrong. I decided to come back to that one later.

As for the Steps in between, the first is the inventory (Four). I didn't do mine in the normal way, but I did do an inventory with the person with whom I had decided to spend my life (Five). I was certainly ready for God to remove my defects of character, just not all at once (Six). I was afraid that if He took them all, I would be like a puppet with all its strings cut. These things had become my survival skills, but God gave me a way to get rid of them (Seven).

What I got from this process was a sense of personal freedom from myself and from the liabilities within my soul. I never have to worry about waking up in the middle of the night, remembering something, and saying, "Oh, God, oh, no." Steps Eight and Nine gave me freedom from everyone else. I can go anywhere in the world now and I don't owe anyone anything. At first, though, I didn't see how I would ever make amends for all the things I had done. Most of the people involved would be dead, and there were so many people I didn't know who had been touched by what I had done, like ripples on a lake after you throw a rock into it. I was struggling with this when the same man who answered the door that first day at the recovery home said something very simple: "One day you will be standing alone, and God will tell you what to do."

Every time I work Step Ten, I touch an old behavior and ask for it to be removed so I won't do it again. One at a time, they eventually fall away, but there are still a few that keep coming back like rabbits.

Step Eleven suggested that I pray and meditate to improve my conscious contact with God as I understood Him. Well, I had already been doing that—I was the most spiritual person I knew. I had glass altars, sacraments, crosses all over my wall. I was always praying. As for Step Twelve, we do this all the time. We meet to help each other, to love each other, and to support each other's need to be sober. I still go to six or seven meetings a week to hear from other members, especially newcomers. My using was a black-and-white film noir that happened thirty years ago, and I think, Wow, was that really me? When I talk to newcomers, though, I see myself. I know where I have been and where I could be again. That's why newcomers are the most important people in meetings. Not because they are new, but because they let me know what it would be like to be new all over again.

In my tenth year of sobriety I stopped going to meetings entirely for four years, but I realized that I had completely lost touch with other addicts, and I eventually came back. I was celebrating my fourteenth anniversary at the recovery house when an 18-year-old kid walked in who was so high that he was roller-skating on the ceiling. He ended up living in the house and I sponsored him. I started taking him to meetings.

Having been sober fourteen years and away from meetings for four, I didn't know speed was still around. Other than a few hard-core addicts, tweakers had pretty much disappeared from the scene by the time I quit, but here they were again in these meetings. They would never get called on, even if they had their hands up the whole meeting. I asked the secretary once why they were never asked to share when they clearly needed to talk, and he replied, "Because they're tweakers and they disrupt the meeting."

I started thinking that I needed to start a special-purpose meeting for speed freaks, but somehow it got bigger. People kept coming up to me, even on the streets, asking when I was going to start the meeting. I kept putting it off, saying that I didn't want to be responsible for anyone's sobriety, but a friend kept pestering me about it. We fought about starting that first meeting for eight or nine months before I decided to listen to the message I was getting from God. I finally put an announcement on the board: "Crystal Meth Anonymous Meeting" at such and such place and time. I then spent the next week stealing writings from other programs to read at the meeting.

On September 16, 1994, we had our first meeting, with twelve people in attendance. It grew into other meetings, then more meetings, and even more meetings. Soon we had seven meetings in L.A., and then a group started in Salt Lake City. Phoenix followed, and then it just blossomed all over.

I have visited CMA groups all over the country, and I have discovered that crystal meth addicts are the same everywhere, because there is very little difference in our meetings. We all have the same tolerance for our newcomers. We love each other a lot. We can be irreverent when we feel comfortable that we know enough about something to make a joke about it. The words in the "Big Book" and "Twelve and Twelve" are just words until we put them into practice; that's when they become a program.

These books all constantly remind us that they are just suggestions, but if we are going to follow the path of the Twelve Steps, these suggestions become "musts." We need these Steps, these writings, and these meetings, where we can come and bare our souls and sit and listen when someone really is hurting.

To those who are new, you will find nothing in CMA but love. It is in no one's best interest to do anything except take care of you and help you get sober. If you want to do it, we can help you. We can't do it for you, but we can sure help you. I cannot think of any movement in the last thousand years that has been so beneficial for us. Thank God Bill W., Ebby, and Dr. Bob (the founders of Alcoholics Anonymous) stopped long enough to listen to their "white light" experience, because we wouldn't be here if they hadn't.

Today, I am the richest man I know, because I can look out over a meeting and see clean, healthy faces that might have been in jail or in a loony bin otherwise. It is these members of CMA, folks who were badly burned by their own actions and who have turned it around, who are helping people stay sober—one at a time—and for that I am eternally grateful.

PERSONAL STORIES

Most of us have found that the more we talk to other addicts, either from our own home groups or from around the country, the more we see we have in common. No matter our background, we discover many parallels in our past, and even more in the shared spiritual solution we have found.

However, those similarities were not always immediately apparent, and many of us resisted even attempting recovery, fearing that our situation was different: We were too unique, too hopeless, or maybe not hopeless enough. Others had tried to get sober, relapsed, and thought there was no use trying again. Whatever the excuse, and no matter our situation, those of us who have looked have found the solution waiting for us in the Twelve Steps.

In the following section, we present stories from members of CMA that describe their experiences with crystal meth and how they discovered the solution. If you are new or if you have been having trouble staying sober, we encourage you to read these accounts closely. Look for similarities instead of differences: We believe if you read with an open mind you will find the hope and the power you require to stay sober.

Personal Story 1

HOUSEWIFE, MOTHER, ADDICT

As I sit down to write my story, it is the eve of my fourth sobriety birthday, and I can't help but reflect back on the person I was four years ago and all the miracles that have occurred in my life since.

Four years ago, I was a 41-year-old housewife and mother of four. I drove a minivan and lived in a nice middle-class neighborhood. I wasn't working because I had been fired from my three previous jobs for various incidents of "creative accounting." But, most important, I had been secretly addicted to crystal meth for twelve years.

I did my first line of meth at the age of 30 as casually as if it were alcohol. I briefly thought about the three years of my life I had thrown away freebasing in the early '80s. But this was different. I was just doing a line. Well, I was right: It was different. I fell in love with the effects of meth. I was able to work ten-hour days, keep my house spotless, keep my husband happy, be Supermom to my three little girls, and look good doing it. Within four years, I had lost my job of nine years, my house was a mess, my husband was not so happy, and my girls were starting to be an inconvenience. You see, they were getting older and requiring more of my time, which I just didn't have. With all the scheming, sneaking around, and covering up what I was doing, there wasn't time for things like parent-teacher conferences, field trips, ballet classes, cheerleading, etc. Oh, I kept signing up for everything, because appearances were critical to me.

I grew up never feeling good enough, popular enough, or smart enough. This was in no way due to my parents. They were very loving and supportive. I started to sabotage any chance for success early on with my pursuit of popularity. Although I didn't realize it at the time, I was very empty inside and always looking for happiness in other people, places, and things.

By the age of 38, I had been smoking meth for eight years. I was getting tired of the consequences, which just seemed to plague me. When I discovered I was pregnant again, I found the resolve to quit using. I felt I had dodged a bullet quite nicely. My kids didn't know. My parents didn't know, and most of my friends didn't know. The ones who did know were not fit to be my friends anymore. My husband knew a little, but he had chosen to save his sanity and stopped confronting me.

When I gave birth to my last child, a beautiful baby boy, I remember sitting in the hospital thinking about how long I should wait before I called my dealer. If I called too soon, even she might think I was a bad mother. I decided three days was sufficient and made that call. The next three years were nothing short of hell. I went from job to job. Stealing from my husband's business to pay for my drugs was an everyday event. I would then have to go to my parents for help to pay the electric bill, kids' doctor bills, etc. Each time, I'd use my husband's poor business management skills as the excuse for why we needed assistance. I dragged my little boy to the dealer's house many a time. I thought I was being a good mom by not taking him inside—I would leave him locked in his car seat with the air conditioning running. I stole from anyone who wasn't looking and felt justified doing so. The only thing I thought would make me a bad person was if my family discovered my secret. Well, that's exactly what happened.

When we celebrated my dad's 79th birthday I stole $30 out of my brother-in-law's wallet. When my sister confronted me later, I did what was normal for me: I blamed someone else. This time, however, I stooped to a new low and blamed it on my 15-year-old daughter. Imagine my surprise when my sister didn't believe me. She knew. My husband had told her I was doing drugs and he thought I had a problem. She said that mom and dad knew—that they would pay for drug treatment if I was willing to go. Well, I wasn't going to look bad to them, so I went.

I entered an eight-week outpatient program a few days later with the intention of getting clean, making everybody happy, and ultimately learning how to use moderately without suffering the consequences. I never thought it would be necessary—let alone possible—to stay clean forever. But a funny thing happened on the road to recovery. I discovered I had a problem, and I suspected the problem was me. I started to go to outside meetings because the program required that I go. At my first CMA meeting, I saw people who looked truly happy, and they said they had made the decision to quit using once and for all. Well, as an active addict, I was doomed; I couldn't make a healthy decision on my own if my life depended on it—which it did.

I kept going to meetings because I felt happy and hopeful while I was there. Working the Steps honestly and fearlessly with a sponsor allowed me to start feeling that way outside of meetings, too. I finally accepted that my ideas weren't working and that with God making the decisions, anything was possible.

These last four years have been an amazing, miraculous journey of self-discovery and acceptance. God now does for me what I could never do by myself. Today, I am a wife, a loving and active mother, a proud grandmother of three, a trusted employee, and most important, a humble servant and grateful member of Crystal Meth Anonymous.

Personal Story 2

CMA GAVE ME HOPE

ONE DAY LAST FALL, AS I WAS WALKING TOWARD THE BUILDING WHERE I was to begin teaching a class that started at 8 a.m., I decided the day had come for me to die. The decision had not come suddenly—I had arrived at it weeks, perhaps months earlier. The weekend before, I had driven to my ex's house to pick up a puppy we'd adopted together, so that all of my dogs would be with me before I died. Nothing in particular had happened that morning or the day before; it was just time for the pain to end. After over six years of increasingly heavy meth use—I used to go through two eight balls each weekend—I had gone nine months without doing meth. But my increased use of alcohol during that time and the seeming hopelessness of my life had made me a shell of the person I had always meant to be.

I went through the course of my day, going to work, answering my email. When I returned home early that afternoon, I began drinking. I wrote farewell notes, which I left on my dining table. In my garage, I hooked the exhaust pipe of my car to my window, sealed it with packing tape, and allowed my car to idle for a couple of hours so that my death would be quick. I had done research online, and knew that most catalytic converters allow enough carbon monoxide to escape through exhaust to kill someone in an enclosed space. I taped notices on my front and garage doors warning anyone entering the house to beware of the fumes. I put my dogs in my bedroom with food, water, rawhide, and extra treats. I sent a final email to a friend in New York who checks her messages early each morning, letting her know what I was doing, asking her to call the police, and telling her whom to contact in my family after I was dead. I got in the car—not crying, not sad, not scared—and I waited to die.

It didn't happen. After ten minutes or so, I realized I wasn't dying like I should be, though I was having trouble breathing. My lungs were expanding significantly—I suddenly thought I would not die, but become a vegetable and a further burden to my family. I got out of the car and called my therapist and asked him to put me in treatment somewhere (which he had been trying to do for months). My mom came from another town and picked me up a few hours later, and I eventually found my way to a long-term care facility where I was able to attend a few Crystal Meth Anonymous meetings. There I met people who shared my experience and gave me strength and hope.

For me, only two-thirds of the spiritual solution I need can be found in other programs—the strength and hope. The shared experience of the crystal meth addict is just different. I believe people who say otherwise have never been a crystal meth addict. When I did my Fifth Step with my CMA sponsor, he was able to share his experience with me—the shadow people, the intense paranoia, the days of porn and chat rooms—and that took away my shame. I wasn't alone anymore, I was part of a fellowship of people who not only understood where I had been, but could show me what I could become and what I could accomplish. My Fifth Step changed my life.

I live in a rural area, and while there is plenty of meth available, the nearest CMA meeting is four hours away. I go whenever I can, but I continue to work the Twelve Steps with my sponsor here, who is in another program. I have found friends in other parts of the country in CMA whom I talk to whenever I can, and I stay connected online, but it is my spiritual connection to the fellowship that means the most to me. Even if the power grid went down tomorrow and I wasn't able to communicate with anyone, I would still feel a part of CMA. It is my spiritual home. The people in it saved my life by giving me something I'm not sure I had ever truly experienced before: They gave me hope.

My life today is amazing. I am a free, whole person for the first time in my life. Everything isn't perfect, but when I see people around me suffering, I am so thankful for the freedom and possibility the program has given me. I have been clean and sober for nine months. On the outside, my life has not changed that much—I have the same great job, the same car and house, and the same dogs. I'm still single. The externals of my life before recovery were fine, too, but I was dead inside. It is hard for me to go a week without someone commenting on how much I have changed—my outlook, my attitude, really everything about me. Today, I want to live. I open my window blinds, and I go outside, and I breathe fresh air, and I am happy to be alive.

Personal Story 3

BREAKING UP WITH TINA

SOBRIETY IS A GIFT. IT GAVE ME A SECOND CHANCE AT LIFE. A FEW YEARS AGO I would never have admitted that I am a gay, Asian-American, recovering crystal meth addict. I am 30 years old, and it took me twenty-six years to realize who I am and to accept myself. Alcohol and drugs tormented me. My life became truly unmanageable when I was introduced to crystal, though I thought I had control when I used it. When I was given this gift of sobriety, CMA became the foundation of my recovery. Today, I am happy with myself and thankful for my life.

I was raised in an upper-middle-class neighborhood in a northern suburb of Chicago. Growing up in an Asian household, I knew I was different from the beginning. I went to schools that were predominantly white. In high school, I joined every club there was. I kept saying to myself, "If only I were white, not Asian…" At 15, I realized I was gay. Immediately, I began to convince myself and everyone else that I was straight. I wanted to take my dark secret to the grave. I said to myself, "If only I were straight, not gay…" I hated myself.

Throughout my college years, I covered my pain by drinking. I drank heavily every day. Soon pot and ecstasy took over. As a result of partying too much, I was kicked out of school. I moved back to my parents' house in Chicago. With no degree, I got a job as a cashier in a retail store. My self-esteem was low. I went to clubs, raves, and after-hours parties and used ecstasy every weekend for the next two years. I was going nowhere in life until the day I was introduced to crystal meth.

Crystal put me on top of the world. I was hooked instantly. I felt so invincible, I came out to everybody the very next day at a New Year's Eve party. Having been awake for two days, I climbed onto a table at the stroke of midnight and shouted, "Hey, everybody! Guess what? I'm gay!!!" I had no idea that was only the start of my self-destructive spiral. I knew I could not *really* handle coming out, so I turned to crystal meth to numb my pain.

Every gay man I met did crystal meth, which they called Tina. I believed it was socially acceptable for gay men to use Tina—I thought being gay meant venturing to circuit parties, going to bathhouses, having lots of anonymous sex, and doing lots of drugs. Over the course of the following two years, my bottom just kept getting lower and lower.

My life's unmanageability sprang from crystal meth. Meth devastated my spirituality, emotional life, body, mind, family, friends, and work. Addiction took over my world. I felt abandoned by God, and I was angry at Him. I lost my faith in everything. I asked God, "Why did you make me this way?" My emotions grew chaotic. My happy life morphed into an argumentative, irritable, rigid, and withdrawn one. I felt guilty, shameful, isolated, and lonely. I did not care about my future or myself. I was unpredictable and unreliable. I'd lost all self-esteem. My body suffered: I was convinced the tremors, hallucinations, and convulsions were okay. I believed staying up for five days and sleeping two days was okay. I overdosed and thought that would be the end of me.

My mind broke into a shambles. I used meth to accomplish tasks, only to find I couldn't concentrate. I got nothing done. My clouded brain convinced me I was sane—the rest of the world was going crazy. I grew paranoid and fell into psychosis. My family was tormented. I constantly fought and argued with them, lied to them, and even stole from them. Despite their constant warnings, I did not listen. Soon I found myself avoiding family functions; I didn't feel worthy. I lost their respect. My social life became destructive. I dropped all my friends who were not using. I was surrounded instead by superficial friends who hung out with me only when I had drugs to share. When the drugs were gone, so were they. I believed using Tina was more important than friendship. Tina was my only friend. At work I was not productive. I found myself arriving late or not going at all and thought that was okay. I was terminated from a job I enjoyed.

Assessing the impact of meth on my life, I knew I needed help. I knew I could not control my drug use, but I did not know where to turn. I tried several times to quit. Even after I overdosed, I used the very next day. I was powerless over my addiction. I wanted to break out of Tina's grip. My life was one disaster after another—I had lost everything. I screamed, "Will this soap opera ever end?"

My parents brought me to treatment on a day in early April—my sobriety date. It was the best thing that ever happened to me. That day, I finally surrendered and admitted defeat. In treatment, I learned there was life after meth.

Coming into recovery was hard at first. I had to ask for help from everyone, because what I'd done before never worked. I had to relearn everything. I had to restructure my belief system. When I attended my first CMA meeting, I realized that not all gay men actively used crystal meth, and that baffled me. At that moment I came to believe that recovery was possible.

Today, I feel alive. Even after four years of sobriety, I'm still on my pink cloud. I've learned to accept myself for who I am. Once in a while I still think about crystal meth, but I now have the courage and strength to persevere through my difficulties without using. The driving force in my recovery is hope.

Having lost absolutely everything to my addiction, I am so grateful my life has changed direction. I am healthy. I have the renewed trust of my family. I am surrounded by real friends. I went back to school and completed my bachelor's degree; today I'm in graduate school. I landed the job of my dreams. I live in a fabulous condo. I love to play in an orchestra, deejay, flag, and dance and have found many other outlets for creative expression. I know I am capable of doing anything.

I try to work my recovery program to the fullest. I go to CMA meetings several times a week. I talk to other recovering addicts and alcoholics. I keep at least one service position at any given time. I do the suggested work. I try to live a spiritual life. I feel so lucky that relapse is not a part of my story—I've done enough research! Just for today, I do what it takes to stay on the road of recovery.

Since I got sober, I have lived in joy. Joy is the total acceptance of the world as it is right now. I am the happiest addict I know. Self-acceptance is one of the most important tools I have learned, but it takes effort. When I was young, I never thought I would be an addict—but that is what I am. I have accepted it. Today I am comfortable in my own skin. I have tremendous gratitude for my life, for my family and friends, and for my recovery. I am so grateful for all that I have. I am thankful my life is no longer centered on drugs, bars, bathhouses, and drama.

I owe my life to CMA. Most of my friends today are in the fellowship. I honestly do not know where I'd be today if it weren't for CMA. There are so many blessings here that I have not found anywhere else. The bonds I've formed, the help I've received, and the love I feel are only some of the gifts I've found—and I could find them only in CMA. With the help of CMA, my life just keeps getting better. I have learned happiness, joy, self-acceptance, and gratitude. I love myself. I can look at myself in the mirror today and say I am proud to be a gay, Asian-American, recovering crystal meth addict, and I am proud to be an integral part of CMA.

DOC'S STORY

As I sat in the lockdown unit of the treatment center, all I kept thinking was, *This was not in the plan.* A few hours before, one of the department heads had called me into his office for a meeting. I guessed that this time it probably would be about how I was always late to work, but since I'd just received a scathing evaluation covering everything from my poor medical judgment to my illegible handwriting, I figured I had better be prepared for anything. I walked into the room rehearsing my excuses, but this time something was different. Six other physicians were there— plus a 300-pound security guard carrying a nightstick, just to be sure I got the point. They told me I was going in for drug treatment, voluntarily or otherwise. In CMA meetings, people talk about the moment they surrendered, but I walked into an ambush and was taken prisoner.

The "plan" had been to have as much fun as possible without getting killed in the process. I started getting drunk regularly during college and medical school, but I didn't really like that I had a hard time remaining conscious after a certain point. During my fourth year of medical school, though, I was introduced first to ecstasy and then to crystal meth, and that was another matter entirely. I could party all night long, then, after a bump and a quick costume change, I was off to the hospital to be Super Intern. I had "edge," I thought; and I had it because I had the guts to push the envelope and bend the rules—which really didn't apply to me anyway.

Crystal made everything better, from work to sex to grocery shopping. I finally had found the piece that had been missing my entire life.

Everything was about power and control. Before crystal, I struggled to make life happen, but with the drugs, I had a sense of instant power over all my problems. (Never mind that I never actually fixed anything when I was high; it was the perception that was important.) My biggest problem was supply, and I made sure I had several sources so I could keep that under control. But I especially needed control over the drugs themselves. The key, I thought, was side-effect management. I became a whiz at "recreational pharmacology," memorizing tables of medications I could use to balance out the shakes, insomnia, and post-party depression. As long as I could cover it up, I could get away with it—so it wasn't a problem.

That was the theory, anyway, but shooting crystal and trying to practice medicine at the same time didn't work out so well. A few careless mistakes here and there gradually turned into serious errors in judgment, including leaving an intern alone with a critically ill patient while I was passed out in the call room, all of which required elaborate lies to cover up. No matter how long I stay sober, I never will be able to make amends to all the patients I cared for while I was high.

When I managed to get to work, I was either blitzed out on speed or crashing after a binge, and I looked like someone who had just stepped out of a concentration camp. When the program directors asked me about it, I did what every good addict does in that situation—I lied. I told them I was depressed or in a bad relationship or just out of a bad relationship—anything but admit the truth. I spent huge amounts of energy covering my trail, but by this time it was just damage control and I wasn't even doing a decent job at that.

I would come home at night and sit on the sofa, watching the sun go down and trying to talk myself into using the "contingency kit" I kept in my kitchen so that I could check out for good. Somehow, I couldn't quite get the thought out of my head that there might be a way to get it all back together again, but I had no idea where to begin. Surrender, of course, was unthinkable. The need to use was so overwhelming that I was convinced the only way out was to die. If something is going to happen, I thought, I hope it happens soon.

Well, something did, and the next thing I knew, the doors were being locked behind me at a psychiatric hospital. As usual, my first reaction was to fight, but somehow that didn't seem to be a very attractive option at the time. I was pretty much out of new ideas, and besides, I was stuck without a car behind a locked door a long way from home. (Willingness can come in many forms, it turns out.) The only alternative was just to go with the flow. I was sure that sobriety would never work for me, but I figured if I let someone else run the show for a while and my life fell apart again, I would have someone else to blame for a change.

As I was considering my plan, a novel thought came to me: You know, the possibility exists that you might be wrong about some things. I honestly had never considered that before. I had always assumed that my conclusions were absolutely correct, so my actions were completely justified. Unfortunately, my convictions about my own infallibility also trapped me on the path of self-destruction, completely unable to grow—or grow up. (Today, one of the cornerstones of my recovery is the willingness to question everything I think I know about myself.)

I finally decided to just follow instructions to the best of my ability and see what happened. After that, things got a lot better very quickly. Those instructions turned out to be pretty simple:

1. Go to meetings.
2. Get a sponsor.
3. Work the Steps.
4. Work with others.
5. Learn to pray.

I was told that if I did these five things I would never have to use again. They worked then and they continue to work years later. In particular, people told me it was important to work with newcomers right from the beginning, even if I still was counting days. I remember seeing people who had been sober for years and thinking, They are either lying or they didn't use like I did. I could, however, believe that someone might stay sober for a couple of weeks. I was able to take a lot of hope from the people who had come in just before me, while people with more time taught me the solution. Recovery in CMA really is a group effort.

Prayer was more of a problem. I am an atheist and had absolutely no desire to "find God." Fortunately, the instructions said only that I needed to find "a Power greater than myself" and didn't specify what that Power had to be. My first concept was my group, since they had clearly tapped into some resource to stay sober that I didn't yet have. I began to see that Power working in myself as I went through the moral inventory and started amending my past. The need to use disappeared, and, more incredibly, issues I had been struggling with since I was a teenager suddenly started to get better without any real effort on my part to fix them. One day, I became so grateful for how things had turned out in my life that I just said "thank you" out loud to no one in particular. After that, prayer was easy.

There was no CMA group in our area when I got sober, which made it a little challenging to find other tweakers trying to stay clean. Several of us eventually found each other and started our own CMA meeting. A core group started getting together once a week, and the fellowship quickly expanded to the point where there now are many groups meeting every night. Now, anyone who looks can see other addicts staying clean and living life—no one has to feel like they are alone.

To stay sober today, it is important for me to keep things very simple. The universe was around a long time before I got here, will be here a long time after I'm gone, and generally runs pretty well without my interference. I have a part to play but I was not hired to run the show. I am responsible for my recovery and a few other simple things like folding my laundry, but other than that, I'm a lot happier when I can just let things be.

All in all, things in my life have turned out remarkably well. I finished my training and I once again enjoy the respect of my colleagues. I am surrounded by friends and have a new relationship with my family, but the truly amazing part is what has taken place on the inside. I enjoy peace of mind, stability, and security, and I no longer live in fear. That alone is worth everything.

What no one told me—and what I never would have believed at the beginning—is that sobriety is not a daily fight against cravings. The biggest miracle of my life today is not that I haven't used crystal in many years, but that I haven't needed to use for that long. All I had to do was stop fighting.

Personal Story 5

SAVED BY A HIGHER POWER

I AM A RECOVERING METH ADDICT. I WAS BORN AND RAISED IN PORTLAND, Oregon, the middle child between two sisters. My father was in prison for most of my childhood, and my stepdad grew pot and sold cocaine, but I was too young to really know what was going on. As far as I knew, I thought I had a normal home.

When I turned 8, I drank for the first time. I drank until I was drunk—I didn't want to keep drinking, but I was forced to by a relative. I remember waking up with a terrible headache, thinking I would never do that again. That same year, I was sexually abused by another relative.

I also experimented with marijuana. Yet another relative stole a quantity from his father while we were out camping, and we smoked all day long. I remember the way I felt while smoking it. It made me lazy. We had planned to pick mushrooms for cash, but obviously we didn't make lots of money while smoking pot.

My dad was released from prison when I was about 12, and I went to live with him in another town. He was into drinking and using. At one point I remember my dad hallucinating, saying that there were ladies in his room. He actually got my uncle and me to believe it. Wow.

I tried crank for the first time around 14. I couldn't fit in at my dad's or mom's places, so I ran away. I drank regularly, and the woman whose house I was staying at offered me a line. I did it, and half an hour later I went crazy with energy. I got on a bike and rode 20 miles. Over time we did more, and I started to like it even better.

After some time, I moved back in with my dad. We lived in an arcade in a small town; it was a major place for users because there really wasn't much to do in the town. My dad didn't want me using crank, so he told all of his friends not to let me have any. But one of his friends let me try some one night anyway, and I washed our sidewalk for nearly four hours. That was a very experimental time for me. I used LSD and anything else I got my hands on.

At 15, after many expulsions, I was kicked out of school for the last time. I moved back to Portland. I still used crank every chance I could: I started smoking it off of aluminum foil or from homemade glass pipes. I lived in a house where we cooked and sold it. I used almost every single day—when I wasn't high I slept for days on end. I remember staying up so long I started to hallucinate. It was my first meth-induced psychosis. I saw people in a park spying on us.

I did anything to get crank—stole anything from anyone. Once, I got involved in a high-speed police chase in a stolen truck. We wrecked and almost killed the driver of the other car. I did some really stupid stuff. I started to notice chunks of my teeth falling out and didn't know why. I remember using crank with my dad and his wife. I hit some major lows at that point. I went to a shelter for homeless children where I actually got clean for a little while.

A little later, I moved downtown. I was off crank, but I sold pot and LSD to make a living. I got with a young lady and we moved in together. We sold pot but eventually got busted. I had to go cold turkey from all drugs for probation. I stayed clean until I was off paper.

During one graveyard shift, one of the other bosses asked me if I wanted a line. I said yes and started up again, slowly this time. I had to make sure it didn't get out of hand. I thought I could control my using, but I was fooling myself. After that I used when my girl and I fought, or behind her back. She didn't use meth and had a bad history with her parents' using. Pretty much every weekend I ran away and used. I started using even when I was with her, but I'd stop at a certain part of the day so I could try to sleep with her at night. It was so hard to make myself go to sleep—for years I used breathing techniques, hoping she wouldn't feel my heart beating out of my chest.

One day, I went to get some crank from a usual source but the only thing they could give me was crystal. I said if it did the same thing, then that was fine. I got it and loved it—crystal was my new drug of choice. A lot of time passed after that, but I have few memories. Well, I do remember some of the crazy things that come with crystal but I don't wish to glorify them here. I will say that we sat and stared out of windows or at camera monitors for hours. What insanity.

Seven years later, my daughter was born while I was off in the woods trying to get clean and sober. I was all alone and thought that would help. One night I heard people yelling my name in the middle of the woods, saying, "Your daughter was born!" I missed it. My little girl had arrived, and I wasn't there. I left everything and went directly to the hospital. I changed her first diaper, and we took pictures of me doing it.

The next year, I got a DUI for meth. I was cheating on my daughter's mother regularly. I fell into my second meth-induced psychosis and ended up in jail with some pretty nasty drug charges. I started DUI treatment, but I wasn't willing to work the program. Soon after, I experienced my third psychosis, by far the worst. I planned on killing a lot of different people— one of them a church pastor. I asked my family for help, but there really wasn't much they could do for me. They took me to the hospital.

I finally left my daughter's mother for a woman I used with—I thought I was better off with a meth addict, because I wasn't being judged. I wanted to keep living my life without being forced out of the insane activities of meth addiction. We moved out of town, and everything was fine for a while. My girlfriend and her son used meth. I wanted to show them how to do it for free, so I spent the money I saved and bought a quantity—and started to sell it again. I honestly wasn't thinking about what always happens. Eventually I found myself at a computer desk, smoking meth and tweaking every day. Right as I got tired of the anxiety, I caught wind that we were going to be busted. I wanted a way out. I prayed to God, "Please help me get out of this situation." The next day the police raided my home and arrested me.

As I sat in that jail cell I realized that God had released me from my addiction—he had given me a way out. After I got booked, I found a copy of the New Testament in my cell. I started to read it and found that if I read for thirty minutes, I could get to sleep. I started praying while I read it. I figured that my life was starting to change. I didn't want to use, lie, cheat, steal, or anything I used to do.

When I got out of jail, keeping my new goals wasn't such an easy task, even though I still read the Bible and prayed. I started to attend CMA meetings, but I started drinking to replace the crystal. I found myself in some pretty terrible places at times because I was homeless. Every once in a while I ended up at the bar drinking—a violation of my probation. Someone would ask me to do a tattoo for him; I'd tell him I was too drunk. Some drinks later I'd tell him that, if he bought me some crystal, I could sober up enough to do the tattoo. I must remember my ABCs: Alcohol Becomes Crystal. This happened about three times. Each time I wanted to stop feeling dirty from crystal, but at the same time I wanted more.

I still associated with the wrong people. I was about to graduate from another drug treatment program and was working a full-time job, but I was staying with a friend who was still an active addict. There were lots of other active users around. I still thought that drinking was okay as long as I didn't use meth. My last night around the users, they were plotting a crime. I'm grateful I'd found my Higher Power before then, because otherwise I would have been right there with them. They asked me if I wanted to help, but I said, "Hell, no." They were all arrested and told the police I was involved. I knew then these people weren't the type I wanted to be around anymore. I ended up back in jail on a parole violation for drinking—which I admitted to. While I was in jail this time, I attended church, Bible study, and AA meetings. I never got much out of that stuff before, but now I liked them all.

My clean date is the day I was arrested—because I was clean and sober at the time of my arrest. I asked the judge if I could check into an inpatient rehab facility, and she said yes. I served the rest of my sentence in a program. A month after I got out of jail, I landed a bed in a treatment center. While I completed the program, I started two CMA meetings, both of which I still attend. I am currently involved in service work in my local area. I also have other service commitments. I have a sponsor who has a sponsor, and I have sponsees. I regularly work the Steps and the Traditions with my sponsor. My whole life has changed.

I see my daughter often now. I love every minute of it, no matter how much we struggle at times. We are working on our relationship, and it gets stronger every day we are together. I saw a dentist who fixed what was left of my teeth, and my smile looks much better now. I have the trust of my family back. I even have bank accounts!

Today, I hope my daughter will not have to grow up in the same way I did. I try to do everything in my power to make that happen. I look forward to owning my own home and keeping a job for over two years. If I can touch the heart of just one addict who is still suffering—and help him or her find a solution in CMA the way I did—then all my own suffering has been completely worth it.

Personal Story 6

TWEAKIN' JAZZMAN

THE FIRST LIE I SOLD MYSELF WAS THAT IT WAS OKAY IF JAZZ MUSICIANS GOT loaded. All the greats got loaded and that made them play better, right? Charlie Parker, John Coltrane, Bud Powell, Hank Mobley, Stan Getz. Or perhaps I thought it was a rite of passage for a young musician to be a drug addict. This was when I was 17 and began smoking pot several times a day.

The reason I call it a lie I sold myself was that I was an addict-alcoholic years before that and had been looking for an excuse to be loaded every day. I was a blackout drinker before I ever took a hit of pot or speed—an ominous warning, indeed. Once I surrendered in recovery, certain truths began to come clear. The first one: I liked getting loaded from as far back as I can remember. Even before I was a teenager, I liked to finish off the drinks the adults left at parties. After that, I clearly remember pouring a little from each bottle of my father's booze into a glass, holding my nose and chugging the whole thing before leaving for school. I was drunk for first-period PE. I don't remember any of my friends doing that.

At high school parties, I was the guy who drank eight or nine beers and was passed out before everyone else even got started. I had a reputation as the one who wanted to get the drunkest the fastest. When I was introduced to smoking pot, I found a socially acceptable way to expand my addictions and be loaded every day. Along with pot, I tried everything else: acid, mushrooms, cocaine, PCP, nitrous oxide, X. I especially liked Black

Beauties and Cross Tops (amphetamines). In an early moment of clarity, I switched majors in college and graduated with a degree in business instead of music. I finished college smoking pot and taking Cross Tops daily. I didn't smoke speed until I was 30 years old.

I grew up in the San Fernando Valley, north of Los Angeles, and always felt like an outsider. I was a loner and never felt comfortable in my own skin—I never felt cool or accepted until I was a drug addict. I never understood how people could not want to be constantly high. I thought being stoned or drunk was the preferred way to be. Being loaded was by far the most compelling part of my life. There was no comparison. As a young drug addict and alcoholic, I didn't know I was playing Russian roulette. I thought that because I wasn't a homeless wino or junkie I couldn't be addicted to anything. I thought I was bulletproof. I used to say, "Reality is for people who can't handle drugs." I think the real truth was that I was a sitting duck waiting for the substance that would eventually knock my socks off and take me all the way down. That it hadn't happened yet was not because of any sort of divine guidance or self-control. It's just that I hadn't yet found the substance that one day would turn in flight like a boomerang and all but cut me to ribbons.

My boomerang was speed. I snorted it several times and liked the effect but didn't like the wear and tear on my nose. When I discovered you could smoke it, though, it was as if all my prior drug experiences were child's play. This was it. I even remember extolling the virtues of speed to my normy friends. Here was a drug that let me work harder and longer than the next guy, plus get the hours from 12:00 a.m. to 6:00 a.m. all to myself to do with as I pleased. Sex was terrific. What was so wrong with this? Show me the downside, I thought—I saw none because I am an addict.

Now, when I played gigs, I smoked both speed and pot. The lie I sold myself then was that I had more endurance and creativity. I met my wife on a gig and soon got her addicted to smoking meth, too. The next few years were a whirlwind of activity; I wasn't really getting anywhere but was still very active nonetheless—getting fired from several jobs while still thinking that the drug wasn't a factor. I was trying to live a normal life, but I ended up being like Sisyphus pushing the rock up the hill. It was impossible. I would build up some stability by getting a new job, and then do something to tear it all down around my head.

I went from job to job, mostly in sales executive positions. I did lousy work but was talented enough that my bosses still wanted to keep me, thinking I'd be an asset if I ever got my act together—which I never did, of course. Also, because I had to keep getting high, I didn't fit in the organization socially. How could I chitchat with people who didn't get high like me? Why couldn't they understand me? I lasted about a year in each of a succession of jobs, the whole time flying into almost every major airport in the country with a bag of speed in my crotch. That I wasn't ever arrested was a miracle. It would have been a blessing in disguise.

I also was chronically late. I never could be on time. I always was sitting at home smoking my pipe, staring at the computer screen, and waiting for that hit that would take me up and out of my chair and into the shower. The problem was that it never happened—I'd smoke until I was late. This happened every day. Another thing I didn't do was follow directions. If the boss gave me a task to do, I would do something else. It's a wonder I lasted as long as I did at some of those places.

I left my wife and started the major slide toward oblivion. I think having to be responsible for someone else had kept me from free-falling in my first several years of addiction. In my wife's case, she seemed to fall much faster than I did. She picked at her face and arms and eventually pulled out all of her hair. That was her behavior when high. After we split up, my home life became a mess. Like most drug addicts, I lived a dual life. My particular duality was wearing a suit and tie by day and hanging out with homeless kids half my age at night. I vaguely recall being proud that I could pull that off. I called the kids "waifs."

I got ripped off so many times I lost count. I still opened my door to them because I was lonely and needy. Besides, these people were my connections. Later on, the feeling of being taken advantage of would help me make a truly disastrous decision.

Recovery later gave me this insight—I had loved the drama. I wasn't one to create the drama directly, but I loved being a victim or on the sidelines. During my drug career, my favorite emotion was righteous indignation. I would say, "How could you steal from me after all I've given you?" Then I would let these people—the waifs—into my apartment again because they said they could get the "bomb" dope. (It wasn't ever as good as they said.) My behavior was the definition of insanity: repeating the same thing over and over while expecting different results.

Quitting wasn't an option. I thought I would use until the day I died. My disease was so strong that I never considered getting help. The end result: I was truly a mess. I used to say that I couldn't afford to quit, that I couldn't afford the time away from work to sleep for a week and stop using. But every time I found myself between jobs, I smoked more.

This is not to say I didn't appear normal to the people in my life who mattered. No one in my family knew I was getting high. All my employers threw up their hands in frustration because I was a crummy employee, albeit talented. It was in my drug life, my "real" life, where things were falling apart. I believed if you kept the exterior clean, you could do with the interior as you wished. That is, keep the car registered, keep working, make all the absolutely necessary appointments, see the family a few times a year, and I could do whatever I pleased with the rest of my life. That philosophy kept me in my disease for a very long time. That was how I kept up appearances to the outside world. But the inside world was completely screwed up.

I still believed I could make the whole thing work—if I just got it together long enough, I could still use and have the picket fence and a life that approached normal. But with each passing failure, my dream of winning in the "meth game" grew more tenuous. I feared I was hopelessly destined for failure. My clouded mind wouldn't admit the entire reason for my misery was speed. I thought if I just learned how to get high without the drama, then I would be okay. Or maybe if I didn't need to have contact with the waifs, then I'd be okay.

My best thinking had me learn to manufacture methamphetamine. I didn't really cook for all that long—I got busted quickly. I never made too much; I cooked for myself. I didn't really like to share. Well, no wonder—it was pure. Not diluted. Just the strength I needed to hasten my free fall into clouded oblivion. The end came when I was arrested for manufacturing.

For all of you who may read this while you are still in your disease: If you cook dope, the cops will find you. It's no joke. You can't win. It's a losing proposition. You will get busted, and it's no fun.

In recovery, I learned that for my first nine years of daily tweaking, the only governor of my consumption was cost. I didn't like dealing, so I was limited to using what I could afford. I had to work to afford the drugs, and I couldn't work if I was up for more than a couple of days. Those two factors held my drug use in check. But with the manufacturing came an unlimited supply of the strongest dope available. Toward the end, the only thing I could do was make another batch. I wouldn't even shower. I lived like an animal. I'd lost my last job because I stopped showing up entirely and they were forced to fire me. The only time I cleaned up was to go to the store to get more pills or chemicals.

Cooking was a power trip. I obsessed over cooking dope long after I obsessed over using. It was a separate addiction I needed to recover from. Recovery showed me how I had always thought I was better than the people who cared only for their drugs. I soon became exactly that—someone who was overtly out of control, a total slave to speed. Getting arrested was the best thing that ever could have happened to me. It was over.

So, to add it all up, beginning with my daily pot smoking at age 17, I was loaded every day for twenty-two years. I smoked speed almost every day for nearly ten years; the last three were almost a continuous free fall. No breaks. No vacations. I had a long road of reconstruction ahead.

Fortunately, I had a great (and very expensive) lawyer and was put into a program. I took advantage of the opportunity given to me to get well. I went to three to four meetings a day for about six months, and then one a day for the next year. I worked the Steps in that time and found my own Higher Power. I became (and still am) very active in my recovery. After nine months or so, a few other addicts and I started the first CMA meeting in Orange County, California. The meeting started with four people but soon grew to over fifty. That meeting is still going strong today.

In recovery, I discovered one of the most important things for me is to be self-aware. Once I got some clean time, gained knowledge of my disease, and understood the power with which I could be filled by being connected to my own concept of God, I found I no longer had an excuse to be ignorant of my actions. I now hold myself to a much higher standard of behavior than I did even before I started using, and the only way to accomplish that is to be aware of my actions at all times and view them in light of whether I am relapsing or recovering. There is no middle ground for me. If I am not growing spiritually and emotionally, then I am not well. The visual I use is a metal ball on a grooved piece of wood. If I tilt the wood one way and then the other, the ball is always moving; it never stays still. That's what my recovery life is like. I think if I stay still, I will lose ground.

Another epiphany I've had is that I can be self-destructive without getting high. This was never something I would have understood under the influence. Relapse is probably the ultimate form of self-destructive behavior. I like to think that getting high is the last of a litany of things I would do on my way to relapse. The goal, I think, is to understand that relapse doesn't happen in a vacuum. If I am aware of my behavior in terms of whether I am in relapse or recovery mode, then I can do something for my state of mind: go to a meeting, work with another addict, exercise, pray.

Being self-aware is so important. If I do nothing about my state of mind when I know I'm in trouble, I am embracing relapse. I might not get high right away, or even for several months or years, but I will get high eventually. That's one truth. Another truth is that I experience both relapse behavior and recovery behavior several times each day. Progress, not perfection, right? It's my heart, my intentions, and (most important) my actions that count. At least, that's the way I look at it. That's not condoning bad behavior. That's constantly being aware that I am and always will be a drug addict, and I need to look at my actions in that light.

For those of us just starting our recovery journey, I think it's important to understand that the insanity that goes along with long-term speed usage isn't easy to displace. It sticks to us like glue. And we feel remorse, anger, rage, and guilt. We feel these things in a sober state, and it hurts like hell. Using methamphetamine produced an insanity that we came to expect as part of our drug lives, and once we stop using, that insanity is the only thing that still seems real to us. I believe that's why a lot of people stumble early on. They miss the insanity.

It helps to understand that recovery is a slow, long-term process. It takes time. We can't quickly fix what took us so long to screw up. Like most addicts, I want to get well just as fast as I got high—unfortunately, it just doesn't work that way. Recovery is a lifelong day-at-a-time journey.

Today, I get joy out of things that I never would have thought would bring me happiness—especially family and friends. I never got joy out of things that didn't relate directly to getting high. Now, it seems life is lush with joy. At around four years sober, I met someone in the program and we married a few years later. We just celebrated our fifth year of marriage and I couldn't be happier. The "Big Book" says that we have a kit of spiritual tools "laid at our feet." My disease is so cunning, I need to use all of our tools, not just one or two. When I was getting high, I had one tool to fix all my problems. I've heard it said that if the only tool you have is a hammer, then all your problems look like nails. My hammer was a glass pipe. Life is infinitely better now.

If you are new, I strongly advise you to get a sponsor and work the Steps. Read my story and look for similarities with your experience. Don't look for differences. If nothing in my story strikes a chord with you, then read another one until you hear your own story. Find your own Higher Power and always be true to yourself.

THE TWELVE STEPS
& STEP EXPERIENCE ESSAYS

In the following section, eight members of Crystal Meth Anonymous describe how they worked the Twelve Steps. They provide a variety of different experiences, some of which may seem contradictory. The common thread is a life-changing spiritual awakening brought about by doing the Steps.

We do not wish to imply these essays form a comprehensive list of ways to approach the Steps, and they are definitely not provided as instructions. Instead, they represent a small sample of experiences in an attempt to demonstrate how people of different backgrounds did the Steps. They also show newcomers to CMA that the directions for working the Steps presented in other writings can be used by crystal meth addicts. We strongly suggest that every new member find someone to guide them through the Steps, preferably someone who has done the Steps themselves (a "sponsor").

THE TWELVE STEPS OF CRYSTAL METH ANONYMOUS

1. We admitted that we were powerless over crystal meth and our lives had become unmanageable.

2. Came to believe that a power greater than ourselves could restore us to sanity.

3. Made a decision to turn our will and our lives over to the care of a God of our understanding.

4. Made a searching and fearless moral inventory of ourselves.

5. Admitted to God, to ourselves and to another human being the exact nature of our wrongs.

6. Were entirely ready to have God remove all these defects of character.

7. Humbly asked God to remove our shortcomings.

8. Made a list of all persons we had harmed and became willing to make amends to them all.

9. Made direct amends to such people wherever possible, except when to do so would injure them or others.

10. Continued to take personal inventory and when we were wrong promptly admitted it.

11. Sought through prayer and meditation to improve our conscious contact with a God of our understanding praying only for the knowledge of God's will for us, and the power to carry that out.

12. Having had a spiritual awakening as a result of these steps, we tried to carry this message to crystal meth addicts, and to practice these principles in all of our affairs.

LEARNING TO FOLLOW DIRECTIONS

THERE NEVER WAS DOUBT IN MY MIND THAT I WAS AN ADDICT. I TRIED everything imaginable to limit my using or to stop completely and had failed repeatedly. Every time I quit for a while, the crushing, unrelenting need to use overwhelmed me. I had to make it stop, and there were only two things I could think of to do: Kill myself or use again. I decided to keep using, but knew that one day I would have to make the other choice.

After a successful intervention by my employers, I was sent to treatment, where I worked Step Three a little out of order. I figured I had two choices: Play along until they let me go home, then go back to trying things my way; or just stop fighting and go with the flow. For reasons that still aren't clear to me, I chose the latter, even though I really didn't believe that they could offer me anything that would help. I figured once I tried things their way for a while and proved that it didn't work, I would be able to say, "See—I tried everything," then kill myself without any guilt. However, I knew that I would have to follow their directions exactly if I wanted to prove them wrong, so I made the decision to do, to the best of my ability, what they told me to do. Unfortunately for my plan, I felt better almost instantly. I have not used again.

A week later, I met my first recovered crystal meth addict. He told me that he had shot up crystal for nineteen years before he quit and was three years sober at that time. He was calm and collected, a professional, and wasn't suicidal as far as I could tell, so I didn't think there was any way he used the same way I did. As we talked, though, it became clear that he was the same kind of addict as me: bare mattresses with a single lightbulb overhead, paranoia, voices and helicopters, and above all, the unstoppable obsession to use. I didn't believe in God, but I didn't need to: Here was an addict just like me, and if the program worked for him, it could work for me, too. That was all I needed to be convinced of Step Two.

Once I left treatment, I immediately found a home group and a sponsor. I chose him because although he shared infrequently at meetings, every time he did he referenced the literature, and since I knew that I would die if I didn't get help soon, I didn't want to mess around with other people's opinions of what I should do. I needed a proven method, and that's what that book provided—a time-tested method that removes the obsession to use when practiced as a way of life. (Who knew?)

I started on Step Four, with pages and pages of resentments and fears. When it came to my sexual inventory, I balked. I couldn't imagine writing all that down—it seemed like forests would have to be clear-cut to provide the paper. A few months later, though, when my sex life was still driving me crazy, I relented and started writing. After that, things began to get better.

After talking through my inventory in Step Five, I must admit that I did not feel any overwhelming sense of relief—just an overwhelming sense of fatigue. A few things that I had been holding on to for a long time did go away right after that, but for the most part, I think the real use of Step Four for me was in learning how to do an inventory. A few months after I finished it, I ran up against a professional licensing board. As it turns out, their purpose in the world is to protect the public from people like me, and they really weren't too impressed that I had been sober for a whole year. They were leaving several restrictions on my practice in place. Furious, I complained about the "injustice" to everyone who would sit still long enough to listen.

When someone finally told me, "God help us all if we get what we really deserve," I ran to my sponsor, and he handed me a piece of paper and a pencil. "Make some columns," he said. I listed my resentments and my part in the situation, and for the first time in my life I was able to see clearly how my decisions had led me to my current predicament. Even more important, I saw the anger that was tormenting me in that moment was driven by my need to "fix" things to suit me. As I talked through my inventory, I gradually started to see that things were exactly the way they were supposed to be and was able to let go of my anger. My need to "fix" things was my refusal to work Step Six: "Became entirely ready to have God remove all these defects of character." I don't do the removing—I just have to let go, and that requires a willingness to change. Asking my Higher Power to remove the defect in Step Seven is the easy part.

I made a list of people whom I had injured in Step Eight and began to work Step Nine immediately. I made my first amends to those people who were easiest, mostly those to whom I just wanted to say, "Look how good I'm doing." I put off the harder ones until I couldn't stand it anymore. (As a friend once told me, eventually the pain will get so bad you have to work the next Step.) One in particular is worth mentioning. Several of my amends were financial, and I was paying them off as I could. At one point during the height of my using, a friend had gotten me a job at his employer, and instead of showing up to work, I stayed home, shot up crystal, and faked a timesheet (saying I was "working from home"). This was my last significant financial amends, and I had the money to make good on my debt. After talking to my sponsor, I called up the company's human resources director and explained the situation, asking how they wanted me to handle it. At their instruction, I sent them a check for the money I owed them, and then waited for it to clear my account. Once it cleared, I had this sudden spinning feeling, as if the universe had just turned 180 degrees. I was no longer trapped in my past and could finally have a future.

As soon as I had done my first inventory, my sponsor told me I needed to keep doing them (Step Ten). At the end of the day, I review my behavior and try to consider what I might have done better, trying to avoid judging whether it was "right" or "wrong"—that is not for me to decide. I have several defects that keep popping up over and over, usually causing me some sort of discomfort in the process. I inventory them and see my part, but my natural reaction is to try to "fix" it on my own. "I need to be more humble." "I need to be nicer to my coworkers." The list goes on and on, but the result always is frustration. I only change when I become willing to change, and I only become willing after I have inventoried my behavior enough to see how my anger and fear always are the result of my own desire to "fix" the world to suit my needs, instead of suiting myself to be of service to my Higher Power and others about me.

I began meditating as a daily Eleventh Step practice during my first month sober and continue to do it every morning, right after I grab my coffee. It really is a "practice," because I use it throughout the day when I'm troubled so that I can quiet my mind and observe myself. There always are three things going on: What I think I'm doing, what I think I should be doing, and what I'm actually doing. It is only what I'm actually doing that matters—the rest is a distraction. I have come to learn that my behavior speaks the truth about what I really think and feel and these are the things I need to be willing to change.

Prayer was more difficult. When I came to my first meeting, I did not believe in God and really had no interest in hearing anything about that subject. That began to change, though, when I saw my life undergo a drastic transformation as I began to practice the Steps as a way of life. One day, I became overwhelmed with gratitude for what I had been given, and I realized the true horror for me in being an atheist was not that I had no one to ask for help when I am in trouble, but that I had no one to thank for the great gifts I had been given—gifts that clearly did not come directly from any action on my part. I sneaked into my bedroom, got down on my knees, and said "Thank you" to no one in particular. (I'm so grateful we get to "come to believe.")

Prayer has been easy after that. I used to wonder where I was going to get "spirituality" from as an atheist, and the answer is in Step Twelve: "Having had a spiritual awakening as a result of these Steps…" That definitely was my experience. It never has been important to me who or what my Higher Power is exactly, only that I remember that it is not me. My prayer and meditation practice is my way of reminding myself each day of that fact.

Without a doubt, however, working with other crystal meth addicts as part of my Twelfth Step work is the most potent tool I have in staying sober. I've learned a few hard lessons, primarily that I'm not only powerless over my own addiction, but over others' addiction as well. I cannot help anyone who does not want to get sober, and I cannot provide that willingness to anyone who doesn't have it. The other lesson I have learned is to share my mistakes. In meetings, I learn from people who share what they did, as opposed to what they think or believe. That includes sharing their imperfections—maybe even especially those.

I have not worked a perfect program by any estimation and have made numerous mistakes along the way. Fortunately, I have surrounded myself with others in the fellowship who, like me, aim for spiritual progress, and we are able to guide each other along the path. In the process, I have made lifelong friends in every corner of the country and have witnessed many lives changed dramatically through the Steps, not the least of which is my own.

Step Experience Essay 2

I HAVE A CHOICE

AT THE AGE OF 23, AFTER MANY YEARS OF USE, I ADMITTED TO myself I was an addict. But even though I believed I would die before I was 25 because of my addiction to crystal meth, I still thought my life was manageable. I thought that if all the things that were going wrong in my life were different, maybe everything would be better. I had no sense of responsibility for the things that were messed up in my life, nor was I able to admit the causal relationship between my drug use and the breakdowns going on around me. I simply resigned myself to thinking that everyone else was crazy.

After I had been sober for 30 days, I met my sponsor and asked him if he would take me through the Twelve Steps. I'd been avoiding this crucial work, but I knew that what I had been doing wasn't working for me and that I couldn't continue to do it alone.

For Step One, my sponsor had me look at all the damage I had done. He had me examine the ways I'd tried to stop on my own and whether those had worked. He also had me describe all thethings I'd said I would never do and then did when I was high, as well as all the things I said I would never do but will do if I use again. Without a doubt, at the end of working this Step, I could see that I was powerless over crystal methamphetamine and that my life had become unmanageable.

As for Step Two, I had always believed there was a God, but I couldn't see what he had done for me. While contemplating this Step, I looked at my life and became aware of all the times I should have been killed or could have gotten busted and gone to prison during my using days. After writing down my thoughts, I came to the unavoidable conclusion that either there was a Higher Power that had spared me during these times—and also could restore me to sanity—or I was extremely lucky. Since I've never won the lottery, I went with the first.

Step Three was not very difficult for me. Because crystal meth was burying me alive, I didn't have a problem getting on my knees to pray. I felt the benefits from it immediately. I had around ninety days at the time, and getting on my knees when I woke up in the morning and saying the Third Step Prayer was a huge help in carrying me through that time and in the months since. When I first started saying the prayer, I would feel tingling up and down my spine; I felt connected. Even though that specific sensation comes and goes, I continue to feel connected. I still consistently turn my will and life over to a God of my understanding, in good times and in bad. Not surprisingly, during this time I began to understand acceptance and serenity.

Having thoroughly worked the first Three Steps, I felt confident about making a searching and fearless moral inventory. I had by now built a relationship of trust with my sponsor. All the direction I took from him seemed to make things better, and Step Four was next.

This is not to say that I deluded myself into thinking it would be a simple and painless procedure. I just knew that it could be done and that I had the tools to work through anything that came up. To explain further, during most of the time I spent working on this Step, I was out of the United States in a country where there were no meetings. I had to get down on my knees and pray every time those resentments and other emotions I had stuffed deep down came to the surface, but I got through it. And if I could get through it without the support of meetings—because of the tools given to me by the first Three Steps—then anyone could. As my sponsor said, "Just do it."

My sponsor and I said a prayer before I read him my inventory (Step Five). With his guidance, I was able to see my part and that most of my resentments were toward myself. I was able to understand that the world wasn't my problem, and meth wasn't my problem (although I have a problem with meth). *I* was my problem. Within twenty or thirty minutes after reading my inventory, I could feel a change within me. I didn't feel as if I could climb Mt. Everest, but I did sense that I had let go of a tremendous burden. At first it was uncomfortable for me to experience what felt like emptiness, however I was soon able to distinguish it from the spiritual void I'd felt throughout most of my life. This was a feeling of freedom. This freedom was completely different from anything I had felt before, especially the way I felt while I was using.

I've always been hard on myself, which made it pretty easy to write out a list of my character defects (Step Six). I also had my inventory to work with. I had about five and a half months clean when I sat in a restaurant and made the list. There were a lot of issues I didn't want to look at or admit, but I didn't seem to have a problem writing them down. At the end of compiling my list, I realized that just by soberly working the previous Steps, I had stopped acting out on many of my character defects. I wasn't being violent; I wasn't stealing; I wasn't being intentionally manipulative. Then something clicked for me. If I do the work, my being and my conduct no longer have to be dictated by my character defects. I have a choice.

Just the same, I also know I will always be working Step Seven. Complacency brings out the worst in me. When I don't take contrary action, I sink into old behaviors and that will certainly lead me into relapse. Working Seven gives me even more peace. My sponsor had me humbly ask God to remove my shortcomings by doing at least two random acts of kindness every day. When I let someone ahead of me in traffic, I become less angry. When I give someone a ride, I become less selfish. Even as I first worked this Step the promises began to come true for me.

I took my time with Step Eight. I wanted the list of people I had harmed to be as complete as possible. I learned from doing the previous Steps that the more thoroughly I worked them, the more I cleaned up my side of the street. And, indeed, I had a lot of wreckage to clear from my past. Every time I wrote, I would get down as much as I could until I couldn't remember anything else. After sleeping on it for a little while, something new would come to mind and then I would pour out even more. Writing with rigorous honesty—and not worrying about how I would make the amends—allowed me to become aware of how much I'd messed up and how much wrong I'd done. With this awareness came the insight that it would be possible to be free of all the guilt and shame from my past.

Then came the time when I sat down with my sponsor, eager to begin cleaning up the wreckage of my past. A lot of it was simple: Stop doing those things and don't do them again. I did the hardest amends first. If I hadn't gotten humility from working the Seventh Step, I surely got it from working Step Nine. Having to say I was wrong worked miracles, especially when I said it to the person I'd wronged and meant it. So far, all the amends I've made have absolved me from the shame and guilt I carried from holding on to my past. I truly understood what my sponsor meant when he told me this Step isn't about anyone else but you—it's about cleaning your side of the street. I have cleaned much of my side of the street and I continue to do so.

By the time I did Step Ten, I saw the genius in the continuity of the Twelve Steps. I continued to take personal inventory and keep doing so. I cannot describe the freedom I get from being able to write out resentments and make amends. While also cleaning up the past, I am able to not weigh myself down with life and my reaction to it in the present. Working this Step in conjunction with Step Three gives me the ultimate tool for dealing with life by showing me how to process every situation that comes along. Ten also has helped me stay out of a lot of the trouble that an addict in his first year of recovery can get into.

I recently started working Step Eleven. In my morning prayer and meditation, I no longer ask God for personal things or for anything specific for other people. I have learned that by doing so, I am praying for what *my* will is, not God's. Now that I pray for God's will, not mine, my conscious contact with the God of my understanding is flourishing. God reveals his will for me, at what seems like some of the most obscure times. I sense a shift, from feeling like a parasite to becoming someone who may have a purpose.

Although at present I have not yet sponsored another addict, I have worked Step Twelve throughout this first year of my sobriety. I have commitments. I have spoken at meetings and on panels. I have been of service, and being of service has been an important part of my sanity and recovery. Spirituality, as I understand it, is when you come outside of yourself. In my limited experience, I have found there is no better road to spirituality than service.

I know if I keep working these Steps and keep being of service, then I will continue to stay sober. I will continue to know serenity and acceptance. If it is God's will for me, in one month, I will celebrate my one-year birthday with all my brothers and sisters in sobriety.

Step Experience Essay 3
SHE WAS WILLING TO CHANGE

I AM A CRYSTAL METH ADDICT. TODAY I AM IN RECOVERY FROM THE NEED to use crystal meth, and it is all a result of God and the Twelve Steps of CMA. I was the kind of addict who wanted to be a good person to everyone else but found myself "the victim of others" and how I felt their attitudes affected my life. I couldn't understand why there was so much pain in life, but at the same time I couldn't imagine life any other way. My addiction took me to places I never pictured I would go: homeless, powerless over my addiction and other people, and fighting with myself and others over my own behavior. Eventually, even my children were taken from me.

I tried to get sober through the authority of the court system. No go. I tried to earn God's love by attending local religious groups and even becoming baptized. Nope, still high. Then one day I woke up—or got up, since as a meth addict I did not spend much time sleeping—and prayed to God for help. But this time, I did not specify how I wanted him to help me. Just *please help me to get better.* It was after that that someone said, "I don't know, maybe you could try AA." I didn't know where AA was, so I put little effort into it. I did, however, seek out somewhere I could go to stop the visions of self-inflicted violence in my head. I was so tired of hurting people that I wanted to die, but I didn't want to leave my kids without a mom.

I truly believe that the morning I woke up and prayed, I was admitting powerlessness to God and knew my life was unmanageable. From that moment, God took care of me because I was willing and wanted to change. I did everything put before me that would lead me to a sober life. That was my first Step One, and the most important of the Steps I was to do for the rest of my life. And praying to God for help, for at least that moment, I was also willing to believe that he could restore me to sanity (Step Two).

I know that God guided me through events and to people in my life. I was led to a lot of places with a lot of really powerful information that would stay with me forever. I was in a detox center when a woman gave me my very first "Big Book" of Alcoholics Anonymous. That was what stopped the violent images in my head. Plus, I really could relate to the illness described in that book. Then a group of people told me about a meeting, which gave me hope that there was somewhere to go so you didn't have to be alone and that others like me had been able to recover from using drugs and alcohol.

While I was in detox, I was introduced to the idea of treatment centers. Having little experience, I made an appointment with the one with the most brutal reputation I could find—the kind that would tear you down and then build you back up. I had found willingness and was trying to do what I thought God wanted me to do. I still had a court date where the potential was there for me to go to the local jail. So, not knowing it was like a Step Three, I prayed to God again and said, "God, if I need to go to jail, I am okay with that. But, if I go to jail, I will miss my interview with the brutal treatment center and have to find another way. If I do not go to jail, I will go to the brutal treatment center." This was how I became ready and willing to start a spiritual life. Whether or not I went to jail or treatment is less important than that I became willing to do whatever it took to get sober and find a better way of living life. God led me to AA and about a week or two later to CMA.

As far as officially doing the Steps, I did get a sponsor and do the First, Second, and Third Steps. Step One was a written reflection of what happened, how I was powerless, how my life was unmanageable, and finally what had brought me to the place where I was willing to get sober. When a sponsor asked me to do Step Two, I was unable to think God would restore me to sanity. I didn't think I was *worth* being restored to sanity! My sponsor continued to tell me to pray about it—not whether or not I was worth being restored to sanity, but whether God could restore me. While I was praying about it one day, I realized that I had not used crystal meth or any other drug for forty-five days. Before I found this fellowship, I could not get through one day without using. I was already being restored to some sort of sanity. In that moment, I felt so much spiritual relief that it gave me hope and strength to continue moving forward. And I continued to turn my will and my life over to the care of God to do what I thought was his will for me.

Now, about Step Four: I have heard much sentiment that this Step is so hard because you have to look at yourself. I'm not sure if it was because my sponsor was pretty mellow about it or maybe I was just ready, but this Step was awesome for me and not very difficult. I was instructed to make my list of resentments, as it says in the "Big Book," and go through the columns. Once I finished, and even before that, I was more than ready to see where I had been at fault. Whether I was at fault in my actions toward myself or my attitudes about other people, I could easily see where the harm in my relationships had come from. Yes, there were a few things that I had no control over, where someone had caused me pain. But remaining resentful about anything would have caused me more harm than good. I was ready and willing to let all of my resentments go.

After completing my Fourth Step, I discussed it with my sponsor for Step Five. I talked about my experiences and how my attitudes and behaviors affected me and the people around me throughout my life. I went home and followed the instructions for Step Six, came back the next day and did Step Seven with my sponsor. I don't know how well Step Seven works, but I pray for God to remove my shortcomings all of the time. I am not perfect today, but I get the privilege of knowing God is there to help me through the times when I need him most. When I make mistakes, I can see my error and, in that, I can make progress to correct it and know that I do not have to feel hate or resentment at myself or anyone else.

About Step Eight: Making the list was easy. Some of it came from my Fourth Step, where I had resented someone and realized I actually had harmed them more than they harmed me. Maybe there was someone I never resented, to whom I knew I owed amends, so I put them on the list. Became willing? I was willing to make amends before I ever started the Steps, so this part was not difficult. I had to find out how to make the amends and which ones might cause harm. With the help of my sponsor and God, I was able to make those decisions.

Step Nine was actively going out to those people and making those amends. I did this in all possible cases. And let me tell you, I am so thankful I had guidance. I was able to focus on my side of the street and seriously let go of any baggage that came from the wreckage of my past. This allowed me to move forward with my life in a much healthier way. I could stop myself from making poor choices or choices I would regret later. Not like using choices, because by this time the desire to use was gone, but choices about boundaries with people and what kinds of relationships I was able to carry on in my new life of recovery. I made amends to many people and my life continued to get better.

Step Ten is something I try to use every day. Some days, I need the guidance of the "Big Book" or my sponsor to see clearly. Other days, I just have an instinct that tells me I have some action to take, that maybe I did something I need to address with God or another human being. This is where I get to make sure I am making progress in my relationships with God, myself, and those around me. When I do Step Ten, I do my Step Eleven, too: I try to hang out with God to understand what I think he wants me to do each day and where I can be of service.

As a result of these Steps, I get to be sober, or recovered, or however one wants to put it. I get to be closer to God and happier with my life. I got my children back. I get to help other addicts and maybe help someone who was like me to become sober. I no longer have to be sad because of the pain I've caused others. Maybe I can give hope to someone who needs hope like I did. Today, my primary purpose is to stay sober and help others achieve sobriety.

Step Experience Essay 4

ON A WING AND A PRAYER

WHEN I CAME INTO CMA, I WAS STRUGGLING WITH RECOVERY FROM A DAILY habit of crystal meth use. I used crystal like some people breathe. It was my coffee in the morning and my entertainment at night. I had isolated myself from my family; I was angry and resentful; I honestly thought I'd somehow been missed when they were handing out rule books to life.

In the summer before I found recovery, I ran into a friend who had used like I used. He had been sober for thirty days in something called CMA, in New York City. I continued to use crystal for about six months after that—but the seed had been planted that day. After losing another job, I made a decision and sold everything I owned: On a prayer and with a little bit of hope, I moved to New York from San Francisco because I'd heard there was something called Crystal Meth Anonymous there.

When I finally got to New York, I had no idea how to find my friend who had gotten sober in CMA or even how to find a CMA meeting. Then, just two days after arriving, I got an unexpected phone call that brought me to my first meeting. You see, when I left San Francisco I'd told only one person I was leaving. As it turned out, that one person just so happened to be on a flight, sitting in the same row, heading from New York to San Francisco, with the other friend I'd met the summer before, who had found recovery in CMA. Their only connection to each other was me. They exchanged information about me and helped me get to my first meeting.

This, I believe, was unquestionably divine intervention. God did for me what I could not do for myself. Faith presented itself in my life in a way that made me willing to move forward in this program.

I came to CMA and worked the Twelve Step program that came from the "Big Book" of Alcoholics Anonymous, having faith that the Universe was going to take care of me. The Twelve Steps I saw on the wall at my first meeting promised to change my life and I'm here today to tell you: They did. In the rooms of CMA, I heard people who had used crystal like I used crystal share their stories. So I did what they did to get sober. For me, it was a problem-solution scenario—a very simple equation. I participated in fellowship and began taking small actions to change my life. I made my bed every day; I called my sponsor every day; I attended ninety meetings in ninety days. I began to see God in my life through subtle changes and little coincidences that I came to believe represented the effectiveness of this program.

Even though it was painfully clear I was a hopeless drug addict, I worked Step One by admitting to my sponsor I was powerless over crystal meth and that my life had become unmanageable. My addiction to crystal meth, my powerlessness, was obvious. My sponsor asked me to outline my "using experience" and identify those points in time that marked my using progression, from the first time I tried acid on the night of the homecoming dance to the last sniff of crystal in the Las Vegas airport on my way to New York from San Francisco. I made a time line, complete with pictures and doodles. The absurdity of my powerlessness was clear—I had never been able to leave my best friend and lover, Tina (crystal). My sponsor asked the question, "If I put a bag right here in front of you and left the room, what would you do?" I told him I would pull a shard out of the bag and put it in my pocket, leaving the rest. I knew I wouldn't be able to control myself. I knew I was powerless. Unmanageability also came out in my writing. I tracked my usage and the associated drama, including drug overdoses on GHB, hiding from the police, losing three jobs, being massively in debt, losing relationships, and, ultimately, not being able to make my own life work. I wasn't an effective and useful part of society.

Then I moved on to Step Two. I came to believe a Power greater than myself would restore me to sanity. Well, there was nothing about my life that was remotely sane. My decision-making ability was suspect and my choices were ridiculous. Nothing worked for me and I blamed everyone but myself. You know, some people say Twelve Step programs are brainwashing. Well, my brain was dirty; it needed washing. For me, this Step was all about looking at the people around me and trusting that this program worked for them. Step One was about identifying the problem and Step Two was recognizing the solution. This Step led to a restoration of faith in my life: I made a decision to begin to believe in a Power greater than me and to believe that it could, maybe, possibly, "restore me to sanity." Today, I know that meant it would make me a grown-up, make me accountable and responsible, and ultimately help me build a relationship with my Higher Power.

The next move, Step Three, was for me to make a decision to turn my life and will over to the care of that "Power"—to turn my life over to God. Yikes! Fortunately, it was a God of my making, of my understanding. I could make it up completely. In Step Two, my sponsor had set me up for this open understanding by asking me to find out from other people what a God of their understanding was. I realized then how different everyone's concept of a Higher Power could be. To work Step Three, he taught me about active and daily prayer—he asked me to memorize a prayer out of the "Big Book" of AA. I offered myself to God (to *my* God) to make me into the man I need to be. I asked to be relieved of self-centeredness so that it might help me serve others. I asked my Higher Power to take away my difficulties, the challenges I have in my life, so that the example of my life could be helpful to others. My sponsor asked me to memorize this prayer from the "Big Book" word for word, to internalize it and make it my own. I did that, and it worked. It was sort of magical, but the truth was that it helped me accept life on life's terms. I also added another mantra to that: "God, keep me out of your way." Accepting God's will is tough for me every day, but it is an active part of my program when I first wake up in the morning and when I finally put myself to bed at night.

Those first three Steps were critical in helping me effectively work through Step Four, writing out my resentments, in a process that took about two months. I didn't think I was angry, but a significant part of this program asked me to clear away the things in my life that were blocking me, to take stock of myself, of my soul. To do that would enable me to heal. So, I began listing the people, institutions, things, and groups that I felt had hurt me. I was as specific as I could be about the cause of each resentment. I learned about "basic instincts" and how, when something or someone affected one of those basic instincts, I developed a resentment. Most important, I listed in a fourth column what "my part" was in the whole affair. How I not only contributed directly to the resentment but what I did to make that resentment live. How I fueled the fire, so to speak. I got all this down on paper and began to learn more and more about myself. I learned about my very self-righteous nature, my *massive* ego, and my fears. I put down on paper how those fears drove me, how my other personality traits negatively affected other people. I also looked at my behavior concerning relationships and sex. I put that down on paper and looked at how my behavior might have harmed others.

In Step Five, I shared all of this with my sponsor, the person who had been guiding me. I was as honest as I could possibly be at that time. He showed me patterns in my resentments and helped me realize that my self-righteousness, jealousy, fear, and judgment had affected my relationships and blocked my connection to a God of my understanding.

In that state of openness, I approached Step Six and became "entirely ready" to have removed all those "defects" or personality traits that were messing with my freedom. The way I became "entirely ready" was to keep a short list of the grosser defects and begin practicing opposite actions.

After getting some practice, I added a new prayer to my regimen of active and daily prayer, and incorporating this prayer into my life was the heart of my Step Seven experience. I asked my Higher Power to accept all of me, both the good and the bad. I began daily asking to have those things removed that blocked me from being of use to my Higher Power. More important, I asked for those things so I could be an instrument of service. Practicing opposite action was key for me with these Steps. I lived in these two Steps and the prayer associated with them at work, in friendships, with lovers, with my family—they became a practical tool I could use in my life.

I then sat down with a friend who had almost twenty years sober and she helped me take on Step Eight. Like me, she had dealt with financial destruction. I hadn't opened bills for almost seven years, and this friend helped me make a list of all the people I had "wronged" and, more crucial for me, all of my financial debts. Making this list was the first part of this Step for me and it went far to reduce my fears about what I needed to do to fix the damage I had done in my life. This list gave me the knowledge of what was before me. It prepared me to engage those I had harmed. By making the list, I brought myself to a place of willingness. It became realistic for me to make amends to everyone, including addressing the financial reparations that I would need to make.

Step Nine was and is about taking action for me. My biggest damage was financial, so I took one debt at a time. I started with the debts owed to personal friends and people I love. I began paying them back one by one. I also had to look honestly at my conduct in personal relationships and determine what I needed to do and say to make them right. My sponsor asked me to be specific with my apologies, with my amends. He even took a look at my Eighth Step list and crossed out some that he thought were unnecessary. He asked me to remember that we make amends to people except when to do so would injure them or others. For some, I had to wait. I had to wait until I could afford a ticket back to San Francisco and have face-to-face conversations. Others needed to be taken care of immediately. For my grandparents, who had passed away, I went to visit their grave site and made a promise to my mother that I would always be a son of whom she could be proud. Today, I am still dealing with the financial wreckage of my past. I took one debt at a time. I made the best deal I could and was patient with myself and gracious with the bill collectors, debt managers, and people I was paying. After all, it was money I spent, it went for things I purchased, and it was, flat out, money I did owe. I will never forget the joy of being allowed to open my first bank account—it took about a year. It was one of the first few incremental signs that my life was beginning to change.

At this point in my recovery, I learned that Step Ten was a tool to help me grow in "understanding and effectiveness." In this Step, I practiced writing out resentments I had day to day. I made amends immediately when I knew I had wronged someone and learned that this was something I needed to do to maintain my sobriety. Step Ten is the daily practice of Steps Three through Nine. It's the practice of the program in action. This daily practice of reviewing my everyday conduct helped me adjust my behavior.

Following on the heels of this daily practice, I sought a closer relationship with my Higher Power in Step Eleven, a Universal "Oneness" that, to me, was about loving the people around me—even if they blocked my path on the sidewalk, even if they didn't listen to me, even if life didn't give me what I wanted when I wanted it.

Around that time, I also got my first sponsee and began service work. My objective in Step Twelve was to practice the principles of the program in all my affairs and carry the message, by my actions, to others. I helped organize a service structure in the New York area, began to take other addicts through the Steps, and did what I could do to help make sure the program that was here for me would be here for others in the future. I learned how to be an addict among addicts, a friend among friends, a brother, a son, a "worker among workers," and a member of society.

I now have an instruction manual to life; I am filled with a sense of purpose; I live in Steps Ten, Eleven, and Twelve and continue to chip away at the financial devastation my addiction caused.

Today, I live life free from addiction to crystal meth. The more time I have, the less I feel I know. But I do know that when I practice these Steps my life works and I have a relationship with a Higher Power. Because I've worked these Steps, I had a spiritual experience. My life has changed, and ultimately, that's all I ever wanted.

Step Experience Essay 5

A LIFELONG PROCESS

AT THE BEGINNING OF MY RECOVERY, MY PROGRAM CONSISTED OF meetings, fellowship, phone calls to my sponsor and other addicts, and spending most of my free time with other day-counters. I was so happy and excited to have found a possible solution to my hopeless and endless misery that the support of other addicts was all I needed to get me through my first months of sobriety. My early Step experiences were just looking at the Steps hanging on the walls of meeting rooms and hearing them read and discussed at a weekly Crystal Meth Anonymous Step meeting I attended. I considered the Steps optional, something I might do later.

When I got past ninety days, my sponsor asked me if I wanted to start "working the Steps." I thought, Sure, why not? For Steps One, Two, and Three, we began by reading the corresponding chapter from AA's *The Twelve Steps and Twelve Traditions* (the "Twelve and Twelve"). Then I would have a "homework" assignment that consisted of writing out the meaning of each word in the Step in my own words and answering some questions. The questions helped me understand such concepts as "powerlessness," "unmanageability," "consequences," "Higher Power," "turning it over," and "being restored to sanity."

When I finished the writing, I'd sit with my sponsor to go through it. He'd ask me more questions that pushed me to go deeper. At some point,

I'd read the Step again and he would ask if I'd done what it said. If I said yes, he'd say that we could move on to the next Step.

These first three Steps helped me get comfortable in CMA and accept that I was an addict. Working Step One, I came to see how I was powerless over crystal meth, and how my life had become unmanageable. I came to understand what addiction means in a Twelve Step program: It's a spiritual condition. As we reviewed my past behavior, I decided that I was an addict and, to my surprise, an alcoholic, too.

In Step Two, I learned that my Higher Power didn't have to match a traditional idea of God. I was told that my Higher Power could be anything other than me. I wasn't sure what my Higher Power was, but I could accept that other people's help, the meetings, and the support I got in the program were all forces stronger than myself—and maybe stronger than my addiction.

Step Three was hard. I didn't really know what it meant to turn my will and my life over to the care of a God of my understanding. I was suspicious and resistant. I went through the process of reading from the "Big Book" and the "Twelve and Twelve," defining the words of the Step, answering some questions, and talking to my sponsor. I said the Third Step Prayer. But that didn't seem to be enough for me. I went to a recovery bookstore and got a Step workbook and another book about working the Steps. I read those and did the exercises offered, but it still didn't feel like it was enough.

I didn't understand that the "letting go" essential to this Step can be, and usually is, a process. I *was* changing, however, and slowly I began to notice this. I stopped getting so mad if I missed a subway train or if there was a long line at the grocery store. I would say the Serenity Prayer and realize I wasn't in a hurry anyway. In addition to the Serenity Prayer, I kept saying the Third Step Prayer and other simple prayers. Sometimes, it was just "Help me" or "Thank you." I didn't even know what I was praying to, but I didn't worry about that. Step Three gave me new strategies to actually deal with everyday life situations. As the "pink cloud" of early sobriety lifted, I needed more than the social support that had gotten me through the earliest days. The first three Steps gave me acceptance of my problem, hope that I might get better, and a suggestion for coping with life: Let go and try to live in harmony with the world.

For Step Four, I used the process of writing out my resentments, my fears, my sexual harms, and my sexual ideal as it is explained in the "Big Book." Someone in the fellowship had created charts with the columns described in the book. I worked on those pretty steadily, keeping it in my backpack, so I could pull them out all the time. Before I got a chance to go over my work with my sponsor, I got caught in a rainstorm. The backpack wasn't waterproof and most of the writing turned into a big purple blur. I was upset for a minute, but then I figured that maybe my Higher Power thought I needed to start over from scratch. So I wrote out a more thoughtful and thorough Fourth Step.

For my Fifth Step, I reviewed my new charts with my sponsor. A few patterns emerged that pointed to my character defects. I had suspected one of them, but another was a complete surprise. The process the "Big Book" suggests for Steps Four and Five really worked for me. In the first columns, I got to rail against the world. I got to write about what everybody else did that was so wrong. And then, with no debate or discussion, column four asked me to look at my part in it all. What had I done to create the situations or make them worse? Why was I holding on to this resentment? That was the hard part, but it was through the feelings of humility and honesty that I was transformed.

Step Four taught me I have flaws, but that these parts of me—which had been causing me so much trouble—were not my essential self. In Steps Six and Seven, I get to make use of this new awareness. A mentor in the program gave me some exercises to do in which I could practice taking "contrary actions" instead of acting on my character defects. This moved me closer to becoming entirely ready to have the defects removed. When I felt it was time, I got down on my knees and asked the Universe to take these defects away. I said the Seventh Step Prayer.

For Step Eight, I made of list of harms I had done to others. For Step Nine, I went through the list with my sponsor. He told me I didn't have to make all the amends right away. We divided my amends into three groups: those I could do immediately, those I would do later, and the ones that

I wasn't sure I could ever do. Now that some years have gone by, there is nothing left in that last group. I believe I can make all these amends at some point, and I have done the work on most. Some were to sit down with someone and talk. A couple were to pay money back. Some are living amends. There's one simple amends I have avoided for years; I keep saying I'll do it, but I keep putting it off.

Step Ten provides a practical way to deal with my anger and spite. I still use this one when I need it. Sometimes I forget about this tool or think that I don't really need to write a resentment out. But program friends are good about suggesting putting pen to paper. It always helps.

I don't remember much about working the Eleventh Step with my sponsor. My work on this Step has been more about my everyday practice. I also go to a lot of Eleventh Step meetings where they read from the pages of the "Big Book" or the "Twelve and Twelve" discussing this Step. The program literature has helped me understand the purpose of prayer and meditation—which I believe is to help me to do the next right thing. Prayer and meditation don't come easily to me. A lot of my praying is informal— just asking for help and saying "thank you." Meditation in which I sit in silence is hard for me. I can do it, but it's not easy, so I have found other ways. One way is cooking. When I cook, my hands are busy and I am focused in a way, but my mind can relax and stop its spinning. Thus, I can cook and meditate at the same time.

Step Twelve brought it all together and it still keeps me going. I had a spiritual awakening—which means I have changed. The Steps have let me keep the good parts of who I am while getting rid of self-sabotaging behaviors, beliefs, and feelings that I thought were part of my character. I now see that they were not the essential "me."

This transformation keeps happening as I apply the Steps to all aspects of my life, and especially as I work with others. This is where the Steps keep giving. Every time I go through the First Step, or any Step, with a sponsee, I understand it in a new and deeper way. With every change in me, there is a chance for new application of the Twelve Steps. I have become a different man with a bigger, better life, and that has brought new situations that demand all the tools I can muster to keep going. The Steps—and the Traditions, too—are the most useful tools I have.

I remember my first trip through the Steps. I was in a hurry. I wanted to be *done*. I don't see the Steps—or life—that way now. I now believe that the Twelve Steps are a lifelong, never-disappointing process.

Step Experience Essay 6

PUT DOWN YOUR SHOVEL

MY FIRST SPONSOR ALWAYS USED TO SAY, "WE'LL HELP YOU OUT OF YOUR hole, but first you have to put down your shovel." Things immediately got better for me when I stopped shoveling crystal and other drugs into my system. But things became amazing once I got to work on the Steps. That's when I started climbing out of the hole.

I have done formal Step work at a relatively slow pace, and I'm glad I took my time. It allowed the deeper meaning of each Step in my life really to settle into my soul. At times, I dawdled unnecessarily; I'm a born procrastinator (literally, I was born three weeks late). And I'm terrified of change, of success, of failure, of being vulnerable, blah, blah, blah. Sometimes, I've done the work "at gunpoint" to prod myself out of some particular malaise or despair. When I decide I'm not too scared to reach for real spiritual growth—when I'm ready for action—the Steps are there, simply worded, and in just the right order.

Some of the Steps have come to me on their own, gifts of my psychic circumstances or just plain time. I came in to recovery on Step Three. I'd been trying to control my crystal habit for years with the help of concerned friends, a psychiatrist, and a harm-reduction therapist. But when the rationalizations and denial finally collapsed and I found myself in an ER—when I finally hit bottom—in that moment of total surrender, I stopped. And I've never gone back to crystal or any other drug. Something magical happened for me. The crying and shaking stopped. I calmly lay back on my thin little hospital mattress and thought: I can't do this anymore. I give up.

It would be a few weeks before I was ready to admit the whole powerless and unmanageable shtick, though I had known in my heart for years that I was a mess, a drug whore, a lush, a junkie. From the hospital, I was transferred to a rehab in Pennsylvania (the name made it sound like a golf course, but it was a pretty hardscrabble state-run facility). It was there that I "got" Step Two. I was coasting happily along on the strength of my surrender, writing notes for a First Step, and having daily epiphanies in group therapy. I made it all the way to the night before I was supposed to return to New York before I even had a craving for meth. But, that last night, all my anxiety about my new life exploded, and I found myself fantasizing about a pipe and a stranger....

The counselors and other addicts had told me to pray, told me there was another option besides chaos and insanity, told me all I needed was the faith that some other way was out there. So, late that night, in a pounding thunderstorm—it was just like a Brontë novel or some noir film—I crawled out onto the smoking porch of my dorm, got down on my knees, and started saying the Our Father (I'm a lapsed Catholic; it was the only prayer I knew). I said it over and over and over and cried my eyes out. And when the rainstorm passed and I had calmed down, after the craving had passed, I heard a train whistle somewhere off in the valley. I was going to be okay.

Now, as I said, the Steps are supposed to come in order. And when I got home, I got to work. I started writing a novel of loss and abandonment and made Excel graphs to chart my rapid descent into hard drugs and to tally my financial losses. When I finally got around to showing my labors to my sponsor (I think I was about four months sober), he was wonderful. "I want you to go get some workbooks, the *Keep It Simple* Series." Keep it simple, indeed.

John showed me then (and again, at Step Four) that it's Twelve Steps, not 12 miles. The workbooks were great for me because I was always in my head, always eager to intellectualize, always ready to cite William James and Carl Jung. I hadn't settled back into my own body yet. Over that first year, we calmly went through the workbooks for One, Two, and

Three; it gave me a humble but sturdy foundation, stripped away my grand ideas of myself to find a real honest picture of powerlessness and unmanageability. To this day, I have a very simple tape to play through should I ever get crazy or have an urge to return to crystal. He helped me make sense of what I had gone through in the rainstorm in Pennsylvania, helped me see that I actually could choose between sanity and insanity if I just had a little faith. At the same time, he calmed my fears that the program was too religious, helped me trust my own amorphous God—my universe that I can't name or describe (he was a Buddhist, for God's sake!). And on Three, he said I indeed was blessed to have hit my bottom that day in the psych ward, to have surrendered without even knowing what I was doing. But he urged me to reach for that serenity consciously, with simple prayers, simple attitude adjustments. I learned to really breathe for the first time in my life.

The Steps are not grand abstractions, but simple actions—straightforward, common sense kind of stuff that I sometimes have no idea how to do. Take Step Four: I agonized over this for about a year before I finally showed John my list of resentments. (I worked it the way it's described in the "Big Book" of AA.) He glanced at the ream of paper and dryly said, "Oh, you're one of those." I'd pretty much written a list of everyone I had ever known and had any feelings about. John encouraged me to cut my list way down. A resentment is "a feeling I feel again," not any old memory I want to dredge up. What hurt feelings still hurt today? That was much simpler.

When it came time to work Step Five, I had to change sponsors. As there weren't too many options in CMA in New York at the time, I asked my friend Joe from Cocaine Anonymous. He was more than happy to help. Joe is almost my dad's age, and a father himself, so the tone of our relationship from the start was much more serious. I think I needed that—I was in a grandiose phase at that point, and Joe was great at calling me on my shit. That being said, when it came time to go over my inventory, Joe was patient, loving, generous. We sat at his dining table for three hours probably four weeks in a row, and he never once seemed judgmental or dismissive, or even bored.

About this time, I moved to Las Vegas to perform in a show. Largely cut off from my support network and reimmersed in show business, a career that had disappointed me gravely years before, my character defects ran amok. The timing was perfect to work Step Six. When Joe and I talked, he encouraged me to take note of the gossiping, the fit-throwing, the sexual acting out, the hurt pride, and calmly ask: How does this serve me? Slowly, I woke up to the fact that I was a spoiled, self-pitying brat. My commitment to Step Six, my general willingness to be a better man, is the best barometer of my sobriety.

Joe came to visit me in Vegas that winter, and we went to a church together to work Step Seven. We read St. Francis's prayer and then went inside and knelt together in prayer. I am still not a practicing Catholic; I still don't go to any church or even call my god "God." Yet that afternoon was probably the most moving experience I've had in sobriety. Churches, canyons, beaches, temples, museums—these are places of the deepest humility, places many have gone to reconnect with something greater than themselves. When we were done at the church, we went to Joe's hotel and lay out by the pool drinking lemonade.

I returned to New York and Steps Eight and Nine. My list was not nearly so long as I feared it would be. At the end of my using, I became such an isolated, secretive person that the main person I injured was me—lost paychecks, lost opportunities, lost friendships, lost time, lost spirit. Almost everyone I needed to apologize to was long since aware of the great change in my life. (This is another benefit of not rushing too quickly through the Steps.) Today, I show up for employers, coworkers, friends, and family, and I think they appreciate it. I've been lucky with my financial amends, in that I didn't have many to speak of. Most of my amends were what my sponsors called "living amends." I try today not to act out of selfishness. I treat guys I'm dating respectfully. I take care to really listen to other people. I really honor my parents and let them in on my life instead of shutting them out. It has been impressed on me that we should reach out and apologize only to people we've hurt if we are pretty certain we aren't going to do it again. For that reason, there still are a few people I haven't approached formally—my brother and one ex-boyfriend. This is a process. I'll get there some day.

Step Ten is not my best one. I am good at promptly admitting when I am wrong—I am wrong so often, I have to be. But I rarely, rarely write out quick Fourth Steps. Step Eleven also has been a challenge, though of course, we get a great head start on it with Steps Two, Three, Five and Seven. I don't have much trouble praying, though I have no formal time or place in my day for it. I try to pray as others pray, using old, old prayers and sometimes getting down on my knees, to preserve an attitude of humble submission in my body. My meditation practice has been informal. In the first few years of sobriety, I started a garden and spent hours down in the dirt, digging, weeding, breathing, listening. Now I have a dog, and I find "fetch" pretty much the most satisfying part of my day. I've tried group practice, as well: I attend a meditation meeting fairly often, do yoga, and go on spiritual retreats when my schedule permits. I'm never going to be a swami, but I hope, as I get older, that I can be a better listener. Once, I wanted to win an Oscar or a Nobel Prize. Today, I want to ace breathing.

I was a fervent "Two-Stepper" early on. In my second and third year (that grandiose phase I mentioned), before I'd muddled my way through my first inventory, I was Mr. CMA: I started half a dozen new meetings and cofounded the area Intergroup, and I sponsored dozens of guys. As good as that work was, my motives were suspect. Today, I try to focus on doing what I am asked. I have just a few sponsees, I speak at meetings and hospitals occasionally, and I do sporadic work on the literature committee. Thanks to sobriety—to these Twelve Steps—I have a very full professional and personal life today. I'd never have time to be Mr. CMA, too. Being myself, sober and reasonably successful at life, is more than enough. And probably a kind of service in itself to the people I meet.

SWEETLY REASONABLE

MY EARLY DRUG LIFE WAS LIKE A RACE. THERE WASN'T A DAY THAT went by I didn't want to improve by getting loaded. And we're not talking just a little buzzed—when I say I got loaded, well, that means I did everything to the extreme. My philosophy was that if there was a substance that you seemed to covet, then I wanted some—it didn't matter what it was. As long as I didn't have to feel sober, I was game. The safety of being loaded and not having to embrace true feelings was where I wanted to be.

Weed was my mainstay for a decade or more, but I graduated to speed when it became plentiful in the early '90s. Speed made my body soar. I never once considered the dangers of switching my drug of choice from pot to meth. I never once thought about the consequences of my actions. Speed made me feel so good that consequences weren't important. That was how much I loved this drug.

The end for me was a three-year binge in which I didn't really care about anything. I was heading for a precipitous fall, but I didn't care. I was cooking dope and had unlimited amounts of speed but found myself very sad most of the time. I made a decision to ask for help and took my last hit. I picked up my sister at the airport later that day and blurted out that I had a problem and I needed help. ("Oh, and by the way," I told her, "I have a lab in my kitchen.") She was a trooper and called a bunch of recovery places and tried to clean up my place. I went to my first meeting that night. I remember being blown away that these people had the exact same problems I had; I knew I had found a home. The police kicked in my door about three hours later. God has a very funny way of making His point, and there is nothing like a little fear to seal the deal.

So when I entered the rooms of recovery I was truly beaten. I got loaded for twenty-two years, culminating in my being arrested for manufacturing methamphetamine. The last few months before my arrest were emotionally painful even though I had unlimited amounts of speed. I'd lost contact with all the things I felt were important and I didn't seem to care. I had played the dope game as long as I could, and the only thing I truly could count on was more pain. I was ready for recovery.

For me, Step One was part of my long fall. By the time I was arrested, I knew I was powerless and my life was unmanageable. My philosophy of keeping the exterior clean kept me in my disease for a very long time. I knew several years before I was forced to stop that the speed was killing me; I just didn't see any way I could quit.

I met happy people in recovery. I saw they had found a way out of the dilemma. I saw no reason why I couldn't take the same path to health. I was eager to start on my new life and motivated to excel in the process. I treated recovery as my job and worked ten to twelve hours a day on it. I always was ready to volunteer, sat in the front row for speakers, and hung around the meeting place.

For Step Two, a wonderful woman gave me my first "Big Book." I remember reading it while moving my stuff into storage so I could live in a recovery home. I had to read by candlelight because the electricity had been shut off. I remember reading about spirituality and thinking, No way. I wasn't a person who believed. I wasn't raised with any religion and considered myself an atheist—I made fun of organized religion. Thankfully, the road of recovery is roomy and wide. The program had anticipated someone just like me and made it easy to start my spiritual journey. There was no pressure: I only had to keep an open mind. It was suggested to me I should "always be willing to be willing."

When I had trouble with the concept of a Higher Power, I recalled a meeting at which the speaker asked the group to help him write a list of the attributes we'd want in our father. The group called out things like kind, funny, unconditionally loving, generous, and smart. He said that we could use the list to make a Higher Power of our own understanding (which is exactly what the "Big Book" calls it—a God of our understanding). Suddenly, I felt included, part of something powerful, and I knew then that my own brand of spirituality would serve me just fine. As long as the Power greater than me isn't me, then I'm okay. I remember being at a meeting on the beach and feeling an overwhelming rush of warmth when I opened my heart to the idea of something greater than myself. Step Two was a challenge, but once I became willing, it laid the groundwork for the rest of my life. My connection with God is the thing that makes life work even when everything seems to go wrong.

That brought me to Step Three. I call this the compassion step. I made a decision to turn my life over to God so I could do His will. To me, His will means compassion for my fellow man. This means I have to love the addict coming into the rooms just as I was loved. After so many long years of caring only about myself and the amount of dope I had—or needed, or could cook, or how a big bag bought all the things, and people, I thought were important—seeing that my life's mission was to be selfless was a relief. Service: That was the key. I also embraced the idea of service because I listened in the meetings, and the point of being selfless had been hammered home. I distilled the Third Step Prayer down to "May I do Thy will always."

My willingness to do everything necessary to write a complete Fourth Step came as a result of being convinced that recovery could work for me. I didn't have to take it on faith that the process worked. I saw it with my own eyes. I saw happy and successful people who suggested that I "get a sponsor and work the Steps." I met lots of people who told me, "Smart people don't recover, because they try to think themselves out of following the path." I thought then, Who was I to try to outthink this divinely inspired program? I think *smart* means embracing the truth before your eyes and acting on it.

After a few months in recovery, I began to see people falling away, people relapsing, people making some money and leaving, people leaving because they got angry at some trivial rule of the recovery home. I watched them go in heartbreaking numbers—and I saw some of the lucky ones return to try to start anew. It was obvious their ego had resurfaced and made them unafraid of the consequences of going out. Could my ego survive while I rebuilt my life?

I wondered about that when another harsh truth came to me: If I had real answers on how to run my life, I wouldn't be in this situation in the first place. Wow! How brutal the truth can be. If there ever was a reason to push ego into the background, this was it. It also brought home how cunning this disease is. The truth is, I might not even understand I'm sick. I might make decisions based upon self that could lead me to relapse. I was terrified of the consequences of failure. You must understand that I was afraid not just of criminal penalties, but also of losing more of my life to getting high. I saw what a waste my drug years were and I was determined to make the rest of my life something great. This kept me "sweetly reasonable."

This was my mind-set for the Fourth Step. I had a healthy dose of fear to spur me on. I thought if this was the way I was going to get well, I should give it a 100-percent effort. I also didn't want to miss anything that would be useful to me. When it came time to write out my Fourth Step, I had no problem finishing. Since getting clean, many of my sponsees have had difficulty writing their Fourth Step. Not me. Putting my thoughts down on paper wasn't easy, but, as I said, this was my ticket to a new life and I was willing to do what the program suggests I do.

Because I paid attention during meetings and listened to speakers who knew the Steps, by the time I worked with my sponsor, I had a framework to accept the idea of personal responsibility. Nothing bursts an addict's bubble—his ability to blame everyone around him—better than embracing personal responsibility. My life began to improve each time I accepted responsibility for the pains of my past. Understand that I wasn't thinking that way all the time yet, but because of the exposure I had so far, I was willing to learn and be teachable.

When I wrote my Fourth Step, I found that the fourth column (my role in the resentment) came to me pretty easily. When I read my Fourth Step with my sponsor, most of that column was done, and those that I couldn't figure out my sponsor helped me to understand. When I asked him about those resentments I'd had as a child, he let me know that I was an adult now, and if I kept in spiritually fit condition, I had the power to let go of the things that bothered me. This awareness was very powerful and I continue to use it today.

Step Five and beyond is where the change in thinking began to affect my life in a profound way. I'm not sure why, but sharing your deepest thoughts with another person is life-changing. All in all, my Fifth Step experience was liberating. I saw—by learning a new way to look at my feelings—that much of what had made me unhappy could be removed and left out of my daily life. The change in thinking didn't come easily or right away. The process of understanding the anger and fear that created and nurtured my resentments took a while to filter through me. Early on, I forgot that I had a tool to make life easier more often than I care to remember. I think pain was my great motivator. It took only a few unchecked resentments running around in my head to push home the point that the only person to be damaged was me. That was very enlightening. The idea of accepting what I can't change is pivotal in gaining peace. I decided to use the tools of recovery to my maximum advantage.

My earlier work made Step Six fairly straightforward. I was willing and ready to have defects removed because I saw what they were as a result of my Fourth and Fifth Steps and saw no profit in holding on to ideas that had caused me so much pain. Also, I bought into the program—I did what it suggested I do. Because I saw the program work in others, I had faith it would work for me if I was open-minded, honest, and willing. Again, the pain of my earlier life was a great motivator. I was more than ready, but I also understood that the removal of defects was a process. My sponsor told me some of my defects would vanish immediately and some would come back to be removed with further work. I looked forward to seeing the process work in my life.

I think the word *humbly* is the most important part of the Seventh Step. I can't ask God to remove my defects of character if I am not humble. I can't be powerful, because only God is powerful and I am only God's servant. But I can be "power filled" as a result of being a humble servant, as long as my character defects are gone. This is the essence of Step Seven to me. I can do His will only if I am motivated to serve and be truthful and compassionate. It's when my ego resurfaces that I get my character defects back. Humility and service keep God in front.

When my sponsor told me to use my Fourth Step to make a list of the people I needed to make amends to, I thought, What for? They hurt me more than I hurt them. After thinking about it for some time, I found I resented the people I'd hurt. The idea of the amends process is to clean my side of the street. It doesn't matter if I had done only 10 percent of the wrong, I still had to make amends for my part. Letting a resentment rent space in my head wasn't what I needed if I was to go out and be of maximum service to those around me. I had amends to make where I'd really hurt people; I had financial amends; and I had living amends.

I went into action immediately. I made several amends within the first few weeks. I had a script I used when communicating with people. I made financial amends when I was ready. I had a desire to tell people how they'd hurt me, but I followed my sponsor's direction and kept the discussion on what I had done and how I could make the situation better. I didn't understand at the time how powerful that was, but cleaning my side of the street would eventually set me free. In my mind, the process of making amends was something I did to help those people I'd hurt; I didn't look at it as something I could do to make my life better. I always kept that in mind. This goes back to Step Three and having compassion for your fellows (and not just addicts). This was about cleaning the mess I made because of my selfish behavior. Some of my amends I made only after several years, when my attitude and the way I lead my life made the change in me obvious. It was only then that I'd reach out, because actions aren't just louder than words—actions scream.

Step Ten is, to me, the most important in my journey. This is the Step where I become self-aware and accountable for my well-being. I believe that relapse doesn't happen in a vacuum. If I am not self-aware, I am lost. I must take corrective action when I see wrong things in my behavior, otherwise I am embracing relapse. I believe in that firmly.

The concept of taking responsibility for my actions—which I'd learned in my Fourth and Fifth Steps—as a guide to lead the rest of my life didn't come to me until some new resentment made me feel as if I was on the road to relapse. I evaluated my state of mind and took the appropriate action to make me spiritually fit. If I felt bad, it was usually because I didn't admit my role in something. The answer was to use the fellowship to get into service. Service always works. I felt in control of my life because I could, with the program's help, walk any road, take on any challenge, or experience the certain highs and lows life would throw at me. What an epiphany! I can use the same process on anything that bothers me. As long as I clean house and trust in God, I will be okay in any circumstance.

Another tool I use is the Serenity Prayer. I use it as a measure of each day. I review my day: Was I accepting enough to pass on the things I couldn't change? Did I have the courage to work on those things where I had a chance to effect change? This is no easy task. The Serenity Prayer is very powerful. Because I say it so many times in meetings, I can take it for granted if I don't apply it to my daily life.

For Step Eleven, I use prayer and meditation in my daily life for clarity and to renew the connection to my Higher Power. It is almost always as a result of some pain. Most times when I am conflicted, it is because I can't accept something for what it is. I can't always see that, and it takes me being hurt before I remember to use the kit of spiritual tools I always carry with me. When I pray or meditate, I ask for clarity. I don't ask for things. I believe I already have answers to my problems; it is my inability to access those answers that makes for difficult times. Prayer and meditation open doors to truth. I have to do the legwork and embrace that truth as it becomes clear to me. Pain comes only when I see the truth and don't embrace it. Another concept I believe is this: Change is not painful; *resistance to change* causes pain.

Service. Service. Service. I find spiritual growth comes with service. After working the Steps and living in Steps Ten and Eleven, I am left with the task that will occupy my recovery life to my dying days. That is service in all forms. Service keeps me sober. I sponsor, lead panels, write material, volunteer in meetings, and serve on boards. I find the greatest reward in sponsoring another addict, but I don't choose one thing over another. I always have my hand up to serve. Where it takes me has varied over the years, but the unalterable truth is that service has been and will continue to be a major part of my routine. Compassion toward others is the hallmark of service; it is the ideal with which I try to lead my life.

Step Experience Essay 8
CALL IT FAITH

I RECALL HUFFING GAS WHEN I WAS ABOUT 11 YEARS OLD AND HAVING A lot of fun feeling strange and out of it. I huffed so much I passed out. I found myself surrounded in hazy whiteness and walking toward a man who looked an awful lot like the picture I'd seen of Jesus. I was saying, "Hey!" but he shook his head and said, "Go back, it's not your time." I woke up on the floor of my friend's garage. He was gone. I guess he had left me for dead—which maybe I was.

I started drinking at 13, and I remember being able to talk to people and do things I always wanted to do but was afraid to try. In ninth grade I was kind of nerdy, but for my age I could play guitar quite well. There was a cool long-haired rocker guy in my class—the guy all the girls liked—so when he asked me if I wanted to play in a band, it was a no-brainer. I learned that girls were drawn to me when I grew my hair long (it was the '80s). Soon, going to parties and getting laid was all I wanted to do. By the time I was 19 I was drinking and smoking pot every day. My mom kicked me out and I ended up homeless and in my first rehab. But it wasn't long before I was out and back in party mode—willing to try whatever drug was around—so by the time I was 20 years old I was shooting crystal meth. I remember my exact thought the first time: This is what I've been looking for my whole life, and this is what I'm going to do for the rest of my life. Even though I was more satisfied than I had ever been before, I still couldn't get enough. But I knew I'd found my drug of choice. I felt like a sex god and was on top of the world.

Eventually I started to lose my mind, and that took a lot of the fun out of it. Seeing laser beams in the sky, thinking my friends were cops, thinking aliens were taking over people's bodies, believing everyone was spying on me with cameras from the astral plane or through a hole in the wall that I could never find. I was time-traveling and unraveling the code in the English language. For a while I thought I was the second coming of Jesus—other times the devil, God, a misplaced being from another planet, and a destroying angel.

I couldn't work because I couldn't think right. Words would change before my eyes. Phone numbers, too. Eventually the friends I'd crash with would catch on and kick me out. I remember going to my best friend's house—he opened the door a crack and said, "Sorry, bro, you can't kick it here." I became the guy nobody wanted around. I ended up in another friend's cellar. I was sitting on the front porch (because I couldn't be trusted with a key) and waiting for him to come home. It was cold and snowing hard. I finally saw myself as others must have seen me, and thought, Dude, you're pathetic. I don't know why I couldn't see that before. That was about my last friend, and after he kicked me out, I was in detox for the seventh or eighth time. I wanted a better life but didn't want to do it without meth. At the same time, I realized that, for me, the two couldn't go together.

I wanted to get it together but I thought, Why try? Eventually I will just do meth again and sell everything and end up right back here. I felt hopeless. I started to look for someone who had been off meth for years to ask them how they did it. I didn't find anybody at that time, but someone who was working at the detox told me, "Get a 'Big Book' and read it." My first thought was, I'm way farther out there than any alcoholic could be, so I don't see how that could help me. But I was willing to try anything. I started to read. I read that the guy in the book had a revelation he could stay sober by helping others to stay sober. And I thought, "I wonder if I could do the same thing with meth?" So I set out to try.

About thirty to sixty days later, I thought, Geez, being clean and sober sucks—why would I want to help anybody to get this way? Then I heard a voice in my head that said, "Why don't you try working all the Steps and then see what you think?" So I found a sponsor and started the Steps. Part of the deal was for me to admit powerlessness and, honestly, I struggled with that because I believed that "anything was possible." I thought somehow, some way, I could control my meth use—the great obsession—I just hadn't figured it out yet.

I looked back over the last twenty years of my life (I was about 30 at this time): all the lost opportunities, girlfriends, jobs, material possessions, and self-respect; the jail time and treatment centers; being broke, homeless, looked down on, beat up on, eaten up, insane, etc. A thought came to me. Is it worth it to keep believing "anything is possible"? How much more hell am I willing to go through? And I thought, No, it's not worth it. Right there, I admitted being powerless, that meth was my master and I the servant. My life surely was unmanageable.

On Step Two, I was hung up. I believed that someday that I could evolve into a god, so I didn't want to believe there was any power greater than that. I spoke with my sponsor and he said, "Okay...but is there a power that's greater than what you are *right now*?" I'd seen evidence, so I had to admit, "Yeah, there is a power that is greater than what I am right now." But before I could move forward, there was more to Step Two: "...restore us to sanity." I figured I was perma-spun and might never come out of it, so I wasn't sure if that power could or would restore my sanity. Someone said, "If you seek, you will find." So, I sought for about a month or so and, in an amazing way, I found and was able to move forward.

I was afraid of Step Three because I thought about all the things I'd done and the way I had spoken out against God in the past. I thought, If I turn my will and my life over to him, he'll have me right where he wants me and he'll get me good. But I didn't want to keep living the way I had been, so I took what I thought was a huge risk. Call it faith. I made a decision and, on my knees with my sponsor, offered my will and life to God.

With Step Four, I was honest and thorough. And Step Five—sharing stuff—well, that made me feel like half a man. I didn't know what this guy was going to think of me, but he didn't try to spit on me or kill me or anything of that sort. We talked for a very long time, and later that night

I meditated on Step Six for an hour. And then, from my knees, I asked God something like this: "God, I am now ready for you to have the good and bad. Remove from me all the character defects that might stand in the way of my usefulness to you and to others, and give me strength to do your work. Amen."

On Step Eight, I added some places and people that weren't on my Fourth Step, and then I started Step Nine. I went to my family and expressed regret at the way I had treated them in the past and said, "If I can do anything for you, please let me know." I began to make small financial amends. Shortly afterward, I started to make some decent money, but instead of going out of my way to make financial amends, I spent a lot of it on myself. I kind of skipped over Step Ten and went about meditating.

My sponsor said he thought I needed to go through the Steps again. I said, "Are you kidding? I'm waiting for my spiritual awakening. I'm not about to start over." (Little did I know that I *would* be starting over after I relapsed about a week later.) I was resting on my laurels; I was ungrateful and angry at God. I thought I deserved anything I wanted and started to go to bars and clubs looking for sex. I was sleeping with women, treating them like objects and justifying it with "honesty," being upfront about my motives. After only a couple of days relapsing, I was already traveling through time and communicating with everyone in code language. I was insane. But a miracle happened—and I got sober with a new sponsor and started the Steps again after only four days in void.

Once I woke up, I looked back on the almost two years I'd spent trying to do God's work, and I realized that is what I wanted. While I was still coming out of the meth fog, my girlfriend—who is now my wife—came to me and asked me if I would start a Crystal Meth Anonymous meeting. At first I resisted, and then about a month later, we started the first CMA meeting in Utah.

Today, I hold this fellowship very dear to me. I can share things people might not want to hear at other places, and people laugh and relate. I feel a lot of meth addicts have found a place we can call home. Today, my life is amazing. I've been through the Steps several times and am on my way through them again. I've gone out of my way on Step Nine. I've been practicing Step Ten throughout the day and Ten and/or Eleven at night. I'm involved in service work and have been carrying the message. I've seen many miracles and have found a solution. It is a journey I pray you won't have to miss.

APPENDICES

I. What Is Crystal Meth Anonymous?

II. The Twelve Traditions of Crystal Meth Anonymous

III. Additional Literature and Information

I. WHAT IS CRYSTAL METH ANONYMOUS?

Crystal Meth Anonymous is a fellowship of men and women who share their experience, strength, and hope with each other, so they may solve their common problem and help others to recover from addiction to crystal meth. The only requirement for membership is a desire to stop using. There are no dues or fees for CMA membership; we are self-supporting through our own contributions. CMA is not allied with any sect, denomination, politics, organization or institution; does not wish to engage in any controversy; and neither endorses nor opposes any causes. Our primary purpose is to lead a sober life and carry the message of recovery to the crystal meth addict who still suffers.[†]

† *Adapted with permission of* The Grapevine of Alcoholics Anonymous

II. THE TWELVE TRADITIONS OF CRYSTAL METH ANONYMOUS

1. Our common welfare should come first; personal recovery depends upon CMA unity.

2. For our group purpose there is but one ultimate authority a loving God as expressed in our group conscience. Our leaders are but trusted servants; they do not govern.

3. The only requirement for CMA membership is a desire to stop using.

4. Each group should be autonomous except in matters affecting other groups or CMA as a whole.

5. Each group has but one primary purpose to carry its message to the addict who still suffers.

6. A CMA group ought never endorse, finance or lend the CMA name to any related facility or outside enterprise, lest problems of money, property, or prestige divert us from our primary purpose.

7. Every CMA group ought to be fully self-supporting, declining outside contributions.

8. Crystal Meth Anonymous should remain forever non-professional, but our service centers may employ special workers.

9. CMA, as such, ought never be organized; but we may create service boards or committees directly responsible to those they serve.

10. Crystal Meth Anonymous has no opinion on outside issues; hence the CMA name ought never be drawn into public controversy.

11. Our public relations policy is based on attraction rather than promotion; we need always maintain personal anonymity at the level of press, radio, television, films and other public media.

12. Anonymity is the spiritual foundation of all our traditions, ever reminding us to place principles before personalities.

from our primary purpose. 7. Every A.A. group ought to be fully self-supporting, declining outside contributions. 8. Alcoholics Anonymous should remain forever nonprofessional, but our service centers may employ special workers. 9. A.A., as such, ought never be organized; but we may create service boards or committees directly responsible to those they serve. 10. Alcoholics Anonymous has no opinion on outside issues; hence the A.A. name ought never be drawn into public controversy. 11. Our public relations policy is based on attraction rather than promotion; we need always maintain personal anonymity at the level of press, radio, and films. 12. Anonymity is the spiritual foundation of all our Traditions, ever reminding us to place principles before personalities. Copyright © A.A. World Services, Inc.

III. ADDITIONAL LITERATURE AND INFORMATION

If you are interested in learning more about Crystal Meth Anonymous, we invite you to visit **www.crystalmethanonymous.com**, the website of our fellowship. There you will find additional literature, pamphlets, information about starting a CMA group, how to be of service in CMA, and more.

SEEKING ADDITIONAL STORIES!

This is the first edition of what we hope will become a much larger collection of the experiences of CMA members around the world. If you would like to share your experience, strength, and hope with others seeking recovery from addiction, we invite you to send us your personal story for consideration and possible inclusion in future editions. Simply visit the Literature area at www.crystalmethanonymous.com and follow the directions for submission.

Note: You must complete the acknowledgement and digital release. All stories submitted become the property of Crystal Meth Anonymous, Inc.

Made in the USA
Monee, IL
12 April 2024

56862100R00066